Toni Morrison's

Sula

Text by
Dr. Anita Price Davis
(Ed.D, Duke University)

Illustrations by
Karen Pica

Research & Education Association

Dr. M. Fogiel, Director

MAXnotes® for
SULA

Printed in the United States of America

Library of Congress Catalog Card Number 98-66564

International Standard Book Number 0-87891-229-0

MAXnotes® is a registered trademark of
Research & Education Association, Piscataway, New Jersey 08854

What **MAXnotes**® *Will Do for You*

This book is intended to help you absorb the essential contents and features of Morrison's *Sula* and to help you gain a thorough understanding of the work. The book has been designed to do this more quickly and effectively than any other study guide.

For best results, this **MAXnotes** book should be used as a companion to the actual work, not instead of it. The interaction between the two will greatly benefit you.

To help you in your studies, this book presents the most up-to-date interpretations of every section of the actual work, followed by questions and fully explained answers that will enable you to analyze the material critically. The questions also will help you to test your understanding of the work and will prepare you for discussions and exams.

Meaningful illustrations are included to further enhance your understanding and enjoyment of the literary work. The illustrations are designed to place you into the mood and spirit of the work's settings.

The **MAXnotes** also include summaries, character lists, explanations of plot, and section-by-section analyses. A biography of the author and discussion of the work's historical context will help you put this literary piece into the proper perspective of what is taking place.

The use of this study guide will save you the hours of preparation time that would ordinarily be required to arrive at a complete grasp of this work of literature. You will be well-prepared for classroom discussions, homework, and exams. The guidelines that are included for writing papers and reports on various topics will prepare you for any added work which may be assigned.

The **MAXnotes** will take your grades "to the max."

Dr. Max Fogiel
Program Director

Contents

> **Each chapter includes List of Characters, Summary, Analysis, Study Questions and Answers, and Suggested Essay Topics.**

MAXnotes® are simply the best – but don't just take our word for it...

"... I have told every bookstore in the area to carry your MAXnotes. They are the only notes I recommend to my students. There is no comparison between MAXnotes and all other notes ..."
> – *High School Teacher & Reading Specialist,*
> *Arlington High School, Arlington, MA*

"... I discovered the MAXnotes when a friend loaned me her copy of the MAXnotes for Romeo and Juliet. The book really helped me understand the story. Please send me a list of stores in my area that carry the MAXnotes. I would like to use more of them ..."
> – *Student, San Marino, CA*

"... The two MAXnotes titles that I have used have been very, very, helpful in helping me understand the subject matter reviewed. Thank you for creating the MAXnotes series ..."
> – *Student, Morrisville, PA*

A Glance at Some of the Characters

Sula

Nel

Eva

Helene

Hannah

Shadrack

Jude

Ajax

Introduction

The Life and Work of Toni Morrison

Toni Morrison was born on February 18, 1931, in Lorain, Ohio, a steel mill town. Her name at birth was Chloe Anthony Wofford, and she was one of four children born to George and Ramah Wofford.

The Wofford family was not well-off financially. At one point, when George and Ramah could not pay their $4.00 rent, the landlord set fire to the house—with Chloe, her older sister, and her parents still inside. No one was injured. Her parents frequently shared the story in an amusing—not a tragic—way; Chloe said the incident helped give her a sense of humor.

Chloe's father came from Georgia. He left that state because of the racial evils he witnessed there. These atrocities were, to him, sufficient reason for hating all whites. George was a pessimist and believed that no hope was imminent for African-Americans. Chloe's mother, on the other hand, was more optimistic. She believed that individuals in society could better their lots.

Chloe's family life had many influences. One such influence was superstition, which figured prominently into the belief system and activities of the family. For instance, Chloe's maternal grandmother kept a dream book with symbols. She used these symbols for playing the numbers. Chloe's father loved to delight the children with scary ghost stories, which also reflected superstition.

A second important influence on Chloe's family was a respect for its heritage. George Wofford skillfully wove the stories of family into oral history which the children clamored to hear again and again.

Music was a rich, third influence on Chloe's family. Chloe's mother was an excellent singer and often entertained her family with song. Chloe's grandfather, John Solomon Willis, was a violinist in his early life and added to her love of music. It is no wonder that young Chloe set a goal for herself: she would express herself through music by becoming a dancer.

Chloe attended public school in Lorain. She was a gifted child. In her first-grade class Chloe was the only child in her ethnic group and the only student who could read. Many of the older boys in the public school were bullies. Chloe sometimes suffered from their racial slurs and physical abuse.

Chloe shared in chores at home from an early age, assisted in the care of her grandparents whenever she was needed, did above-average school work, and worked for other families from the time she was 12. Although her employers could be cruel to her, her father reminded her that she did not live there. Her father told her to do the work and come on home; Chloe learned not to let others determine her feelings about herself.

Chloe attended high school in Lorain. She studied hard, was a member of the honor society, worked outside the home, and still found time to read the great novels of Russia, France, England, and America. Chloe graduated from Lorain High School in 1949.

Chloe was admitted to Howard University in Washington, DC. Chloe's parents recognized the intelligence of their daughter and wanted to help her succeed. Her father worked three jobs simultaneously to help pay her way; her mother took a job as a restroom attendant.

At Howard, Chloe's classmates recognized Chloe as an actress. She traveled with the Howard University Players and visited the South for the first time with this traveling group. Drama became important to her.

Chloe majored in literature. During her college years, she changed her name to Toni. In 1953 she received a B.A. in English, and in 1955 she earned an M.A. from Cornell. Her thesis topic was *Suicide in Faulkner and Woolf.*

Toni accepted a teaching position at Texas Southern University in Houston, Texas. She went back to Howard as an instructor in English and the humanities; there, she assumed many duties, teaching general composition and literature classes while serving as faculty adviser to the English Club. Toni lectured on prominent black rights activists, such as Stokeley Carmichael and Claude Brown while she was at Howard. Brown brought her an 800-page manuscript to critique; this manuscript became *Manchild in the Promised Land*, a novel hailed as a modern classic.

Toni joined a group of writers and poets with monthly meetings. At every session they each shared something they had written. When Toni used up all her high school writings, she wrote a story of a little black girl wishing for blue eyes. She took the idea from an emotional, real-life event. This was the beginning of her first novel and her life as a writer.

Toni met and married Harold Morrison, a Jamaican architecture student, in 1957. In 1964 she left her job at Howard. She and Harold went to Europe with their young son, Ford. While in Europe, Harold and Toni separated. Toni was pregnant with their second child.

With Ford, Toni returned to family and friends in Lorain. After her second child, Slade, was born, Toni moved to Syracuse to become an editor for I. W. Singer Publishing House, a subsidiary of Random House.

Within two years Toni moved from textbook editor to trade editor. By 1967 she was Senior Editor at Random House in New York City, where she encouraged the publication of many new writers—particularly those writing about the black culture. She edited an autobiography by Angela Davis and another by Muhammad Ali.

After working all day and spending time with her boys every evening, Toni sat down alone each night to work on her own book about the little girl who wanted blue eyes. *The Bluest Eye* (1970) was Toni's first novel. Her second novel was *Sula* (1973). Morrison found that when her children were growing up, it was easier to write in the family room with them around; she learned to tune out noise as she wrote.

In 1974, Random House published *The Black Book*, a collection of African-American culture, life, history, and narratives. Although her name did not appear as the creator, Morrison was the driving force behind publication of the book. During her research for *The Black Book*, she found the story of Margaret Garner, an escaped slave who tried to kill her children so that they would not lose their freedom. This story became the basis of her much later novel *Beloved* (1987).

Morrison began teaching creative writing and African-American studies at Yale. Her novel *Song of Solomon* (1977) received the National Book Critics Circle Award and also the American Academy and Institute of Arts and Letters Award. Because her books were becoming best sellers, she was able to buy a three-story home for her family. Morrison's *Tar Baby* appeared in print in 1981, and as a result of her recognition, she became the cover story for *Newsweek*.

Morrison was always working. She took a position as Associate Professor at SUNY Purchase and Bard College in New York. In 1984 she resigned her job at Random House and became the Albert Schweitzer Professor of Humanities at State University of New York at Albany. She wrote her first play while she was there.

On April 1, 1988, Morrison won the Pulitzer Prize for fiction. Morrison made it clear to her public that how she was ranked did not change her life. She was not writing for accolades or wealth. She wrote to satisfy herself first. Her popularity grew as more and more readers discovered her writings.

In 1992, her book *Jazz* appeared in print. In the same year, her collection of essays, titled *Playing in the Dark: Whiteness and the Literary Imagination*, was published. Morrison found time to edit and contribute to another book of essays, *Race-ing Justice, En-Gendering Power: Essays on Anita Hill, Clarence Thomas, and the Construction of Social Reality.*

Other honors followed. In October of 1993 Toni won the Nobel Prize for literature. She traveled to Stockholm, Sweden, in December to receive the coveted award. Reporters and the general public received her acceptance speech with acclaim.

Only a few days after her return from Sweden, a Christmas fire destroyed Morrison's Hudson River home. Over 100 firefighters fought the blaze to no avail. Morrison lost much memorabilia in the fire.

She was acquiring new treasures, however. In 1995 she attended the dedication of the Toni Morrison Reading Room in the Lorain Public Library, and she received a Matrix Award and the title Doctor of Humane Letters from Howard University.

But Morrison's work is not done yet. Her literature, like her life, continues to enrich the lives of readers everywhere.

Historical Background

Sula is set in Medallion, Ohio. This small town with its close relationships among the neighbors essentially has two segments: the valley where the whites live and the Bottom where the blacks reside. Because Medallion figures prominently into the plot and because the geographic location and the physical features described in *Sula* are unique to Ohio, the setting is integral to—not a backdrop to—the action. The hills and the valley serve to clarify the conflicts and to illuminate the characters; these two features are a literal—not a figurative—part of the text.

The first date in the chapter titles is 1919, and the last date is 1965. However, *Sula* is nonchronological; the chapters do not progress sequentially as the reader might expect. In her writing Morrison predicts a time after the 1965 date and takes the reader to the time of slavery—many years before 1919. Her depiction of a socially and racially divided town helps the reader to understand life in a small town in an earlier era.

Master List of Characters

Sula Peace—*a little girl who grows into a woman in the Bottom; the best friend of Nel; granddaughter of Eva; daughter of Hannah.*

Inhabitants of the Bottom—*black people who live in the hills and are dissatisfied with their lots.*

Inhabitants of the valley—*white people who live in the valley.*

Slave owner—*man who gives his slave a chore with the promise of freedom and a parcel of land upon successful completion; talks the slave into taking hill land instead of fertile valley; says that the hill land is the bottom of Heaven.*

Slave—*performs the chores given to him and accepts the Bottom parcel of land.*

Shadrack—*a young man with a psychological war injury from World War I; founder of National Suicide Day.*

Male nurse—*the balding man who treats Shadrack in the hospital.*

Reverend Deal—*a minister of the Bottom who accepts National Suicide Day.*

Cecile—*great aunt to Wiley Wright and grandmother to Helene; took Helene from the Sundown House and reared her in New Orleans.*

Helene Sabat—*daughter of a Creole prostitute; born behind the red shutters of Sundown House.*

Wiley Wright— *nephew of Cecile; resided in Medallion, Ohio; married Helene Sabat, when she was 16; a seaman in port only three days out of every 16; served as cook aboard the ship.*

Nel—*the daughter of Helene and Wiley Wright after their ninth year of marriage.*

Henri Martin—*New Orleans resident who writes to Helene to tell her of her grandmother's illness.*

Porter—*the colored man who points Helene and Nel to the coach.*

Conductor—*the white man who calls Helene "gal" and who questions Helene's and Nel's presence in the white section of the coach.*

Black woman and her four children—*passengers who boarded in Tuscaloosa; the woman shows Helene and Nel the field that is used for a restroom.*

Rochelle—*Helene's mother and Nel's grandmother.*

Eva—*Sula's grandmother.*

Hannah—*Sula's mother; Eva's oldest child.*

BoyBoy—*Eva's husband and Sula's grandfather.*

Pearl—*Eva's daughter; real name is Eva; younger than Hannah; aunt of Sula; married at 14 and moved to Flint, Michigan.*

Plum—*Eva's son; real name is Ralph.*

Suggs family—*gave food to Eva and her children; gave castor oil to Eva when Plum was constipated; poured water on Hannah when fire consumed her.*

Mr. and Mrs. Jackson—*gave milk to Eva and her children.*

Eva's adopted children—*all three named dewey; one with red hair and freckles, one perhaps half-Mexican, one deeply black; no individuality of mind.*

Rekus—*husband of Hannah; father of Sula; died when Sula was three.*

Tar Baby—*along with the deweys, first to follow Shadrack; came in 1920; had some—or all—white blood; mountain boy; alcoholic.*

Mrs. Reed—*teacher; gave all three deweys the last name of King and the same age.*

Buckland Reed—*husband of the teacher, Mrs. Reed; takes numbers from the residents of the Bottom; makes a comment about Eva's leg being worth $10,000.*

Ajax—*21-year-old man with sinister beauty; a frequenter of the pool halls; calls Sula "pig meat" when he sees her; Sula's lover.*

Chicken Little—*a little boy whom Sula swings around; drowns when he slips from Sula's hands and goes into the lake.*

Patsy and Valentine—*Hannah's two friends who are visiting with her the day Chicken Little drowned.*

Four white, Irish boys—*newly arrived residents of the Bottom; taunted the girls.*

Bargeman—*the one who found Chicken Little's body.*

Iceman—*delivers ice to the homes.*

Willy Fields—*orderly who saved Eva from bleeding to death and received her curse for doing so the rest of her life.*

Jude Greene—*tenor in Mt. Zion's Men Quartet; 20-year-old bridegroom of Nel Wright; waiter at Hotel Medallion; leaves with Sula.*

John L. and Shirley—*a couple Sula and Nel remember from their youth.*

Laura—*the helper who had been living with Eva, Sula, the deweys, and Tar Baby.*

Mrs. Rayford—*the next-door neighbor to Nel and Jude.*

Teapot—*five-year-old son of Betty.*

Betty—*often called Teapot's Mama because mothering was her major failure in life; reforms and becomes a good mother for a while; however, she relapses and fails at mothering again.*

Mr. Finley—*was sucking on a chicken bone when he saw Sula and choked.*

Dessie—*Big Daughter Elk; saw Shadrack tip his imaginary hat to Sula and developed a sty on her eye afterward.*

Ivy and Cora—*Dessie's friends.*

Ajax's mother—*the only thing Ajax had ever loved besides airplanes.*

Nathan—*the school-age child who checks on Sula and runs errands for her periodically; discovers her lifeless body.*

Mr. Hodges—*man who hires Shadrack to rake leaves; Shadrack becomes aware of Sula's death when he sees her on a table at Hodges' home.*

L.P., Paul Freeman and his brother Jake, Mrs. Scott's twins—*examples of the beautiful boys of 1921.*

Summary of the Novel

Sula is a multi-faceted novel. It is, first of all, a story of the friendship of two black women (Sula and Nel) over a period of almost 45 years. The friendship, which begins in about 1921, continues through high school and even until Nel's marriage to Jude.

It is almost ten years after Nel's marriage before Sula returns to the small town of Medallion, Ohio; she brings home tales of college and travels. When Nel meets Sula again, their friendship commences as if nothing had ever happened. Nel, however, interrupts Sula and Jude as they are having sex. Jude and Sula leave town together, but Sula soon returns alone. Nel has no contact with Sula for three more years.

Nel goes to Sula when she finds out that Sula is dying. Sula tells Nel that if Nel had truly loved her, Nel would have forgiven her. Nel still does not forgive and continues to ask why Sula behaved as she did. It is only after Sula's death and burial that Nel realizes that it has been Sula—not Jude—whom Nel has missed through the years.

Sula is also the story of a neighborhood. The Bottom (actually the hilly land which is supposed to be the bottom of Heaven) with its black residents and the valley with its white residents are marked contrasts. Neither group of inhabitants seems content. The valley residents eventually take over much of the Bottom. The tight-knit neighborhood of the Bottom changes into a community where the people seek little connection with one another. The Bottom residents themselves destroy the uncompleted tunnel, a link to future employment and travel opportunities.

Sula traces family histories from grandparents, parents, Nel and Sula themselves, and Nel's family. Interwoven with their lives are Shadrack, who suffers with a psychological injury from the war, the adopted deweys, and the Jackson and Suggs families.

Sula is a tragedy which unfolds in nonchronological order. Sula's mother burns to death in her sight, her uncle burns at the hand of his mother (Sula's grandmother), and Sula dies alone at a young age. Shadrack's life is never the same after World War I. Nel spends her adult years as a single mother rearing three children and mourning the loss of a husband—and later a friend. Eva engages in self-mutilation and loses a leg to draw insurance money, sets fire to her own son, sees her daughter burn to death, and, at last, must reside in an old age home at the hand of her granddaughter. Jude loses his wife and three children when he has sex with his wife's best friend. The community residents, who had been close, separate themselves from one another; they eventually destroy the tunnel—their link to the New Road and to promised employment opportunities. Many people die in the destruction. Hate, sarcasm, loss of life, and lack of identity bring unhappiness to an area which is supposed to be the Bottom of Heaven.

Marvin, in *Library Journal* of 1973, calls *Sula* "an evocation of a whole black community during a span of over 40 years." Morrison, he says, describes this "re-creation of the black experience in

America with both artistry and authenticity." In the *New York Times Book Review,* Blackburn describes the novel as "frozen" and "stylized." She calls it an "icy version" of Morrison's first novel and a book with characters who are "achingly alive." Prescott in *Newsweek* of 1974 calls *Sula* an "exemplary fable...arranged in a pattern that cannot be anticipated until the author is done with her surprises." Prescott comments on the "surprising scope and depth" of *Sula*; Blackburn calls it a "howl of love and rage."

Estimated Reading Time

The average silent reading rate for a secondary student is 250 to 300 words per minute, according to Lambert. Because each page has about 300 words on it, an average student would take about one minute to read each page. The reading time for the 174-page book would be about three hours. One must, however, allow extra time for interpretation. This means that the total reading time for *Sula* will probably be about four hours. Reading the book according to the natural chapter breaks is the best approach.

SECTION TWO

Part One

Introduction

New Characters:

Sula Peace: *a little girl who grows into a woman in the Bottom*

Inhabitants of the Bottom: *black people who live in the hills and are dissatisfied with their lots*

Inhabitants of the valley: *white people who live in the valley*

Slave owner: *man who gives his slave a chore with the promise of both freedom and a parcel of land upon successful completion; talks the slave into taking hill land instead; says that the hill land is the bottom of Heaven*

Slave: *performs the chores given to him and accepts the Bottom parcel of land*

Summary

The Medallion City Golf Course and the suburbs were replacing beech trees, the blossoming pear trees with children in their branches, the Time and a Half Pool Hall, Irene's Palace of Cosmetology, Reba's Grill, and the old neighborhood.

The white people lived in the rich valley because of a slave owner's trickery. The slave owner promised his slave a parcel of land and freedom if he performed some difficult tasks. After accomplishing the tasks, the slave was given his freedom, but the owner was reluctant to give him a parcel of land. Instead, the owner tried to outwit the worker by telling him that the hills were the bottom of Heaven. The ex-slave innocently asked for the Bottom, and the owner gave him the land. Since that time the ex-slave and, later, his descendants, had to work hard on hilly land. Plowing was difficult. Soil and seeds washed away. The wind blew.

Later, the white people in the valley decided that they liked the hills, the view, and the sounds of laughter, banjos, and song they heard coming from the Bottom. A visitor to the hills might see a woman dancing to the music from a mouth organ and the watchers laughing. Such a stranger might question if the slave owner had been right in his verbal appraisal of the hills. A hunter might wonder if the Bottom were not better than the valley. Even though the residents of the Bottom had little time to consider it, they would quickly respond that the valley was better.

Analysis

The theme of discontent with one's lot in life is obvious throughout the chapter. The hilly land becomes the reward for the ex-slave; the worker trustingly accepts the word of the farmer that the hills are superior to the valley. The hill residents soon become disillusioned with the acreage that they have accepted and envy the land of the valley residents. On the other hand, the inhabitants of the low lands often view with envy the neighborhood that they can see and hear above them.

Pronounced change is assaulting Medallion. The Bottom in particular, the narrator tells us, is changing quite rapidly. The Medallion City Golf Course and the suburbs are replacing the woods and the buildings in the old neighborhood. The residents of the Bottom, however, remain innocent and totally unaware of the value of what they possess. Even the threat of losing what they own does not bring an awareness to the hill residents. The result of the change is lost on the innocent hill residents.

It is evident that the setting is integral to the plot; it also serves to illuminate the characters and clarify the conflict. The setting suggests the idea of Heaven and Hell. The Bottom does indeed resemble Heaven, the residents look down on the white people

below, and the innocence of the people suggests their goodness. The inhabitants of the Bottom, however, often ignore the beauty and their good fortune to be there.

Innocence is a major theme in this chapter. The slave trustingly accepts the story of his owner about the Bottom. The slave owner takes advantage of the naiveté of the slave and uses the slave's trusting nature to his own advantage. He has deliberately used deceit. The residents of the Bottom are also innocent in that they do not realize the value of their land and their culture.

It is at this point that *Sula* departs from the stories one usually reads. There are no rewards for the goodness and innocence of the slave; there is no punishment evident for the evil acts of the slave owner. The separation of the whites and the blacks continues over several generations, and both parties maintain their discontent.

The slaves and their descendants seem unaware of the value of their possessions; they desire the valley. The valley dwellers continue to be greedy and cling to what they have—while wanting what the Bottom dwellers have also. Every indication is that the valley residents will take over the hill land and displace the residents there without any punishment for their greed and deceit.

It is significant that both good and evil are in the story. The blacks on the hilly land accept the fact that both right and wrong exist, but they do not try to change things. Even when the townspeople of Medallion, Ohio, spread their golf course and suburbs into the Bottom and raze, or tear down, the buildings there, the inhabitants of the Bottom do not protest. These hill inhabitants see evil merely as something that they must withstand or bear and not as something they must eliminate or change. Retaliation for wrongs inflicted on them or on their ancestors is something that the hill residents do not consider. They do not demand rewards for their tenacity or punishment for the wicked.

The characters in the chapter are flat characters. Morrison does not try to make them complete to the reader by revealing their thoughts, their actions, their speech, or their personal history. Rather Morrison presents them as a stereotypical slave owner with only his own interests at heart and a slave, who is innocent and often misled by one who pretends to have his best interests at heart.

The stereotypical view of the easily-duped slave seems to persist into the twentieth century with the innocent Bottom residents.

Morrison makes use of many stylistic devices in depicting the Bottom. Alliteration is evident in "…a bit of cakewalk, a bit of black bottom, a bit of 'messing around'… ." She effectively uses contrasts: white vs. black, hills vs. valley, slave owner vs. slave, trickster vs. tricked, innocent vs. guilty. Personification pictures fingers which dance on the wood and kiss skin. Very descriptive language allows the reader to see both the streets of Medallion which were "hot and dusty with progress" and the heavy trees sheltering the shacks in the Bottom.

Morrison does not use a simple chronological order for the plot of this chapter—or for the entire book. Rather she weaves the plot through the use of foreshadowing, flashbacks, and chronological development. The plot spirals, doubles back, and skips forward. Such plot development allows the narrator much leeway in telling the story and makes it necessary for the readers to attend carefully to the detail to ensure that they receive all the information correctly.

With such an eclectic order in the plot, the writer can leave the reader hanging and answer the questions at a later point in the narrative; the writer does not have to systematically answer the posed questions in chronological order. Waiting for the answers creates suspense for the reader.

Unanswered questions at the end of the introduction entice the reader to continue the book. The unanswered questions in this first part of *Sula* include what Shadrack is all about, what Sula is all about, and who the black people really are. It is evident, then, that *Sula* is not episodic. Rather, *Sula* is a suspenseful novel which requires the reader to complete the entire book to answer all the questions.

Study Questions

1. What was the name of the town near the Bottom?
2. Where was the town?
3. What grew on the Bottom before the spread of the town?

4. What were the names of the three businesses that the white townspeople planned to destroy?

5. What does the word *raze* mean?

6. What were the two rewards the white slave owner promised the slave for completing the chores?

7. What was the name of the hilly land where the black people lived?

8. How did the hilly land get its name?

9. Who was the little girl introduced in the chapter who grew into a woman in the Bottom?

10. What did the white people below think about the hilly land?

Answers

1. The name of the town was Medallion.

2. The town was in a valley in Ohio.

3. Before the spread of the town, trees grew on the Bottom.

4. The names of the three businesses that the townspeople planned to destroy were Reba's Grill, the Time and a Half Pool Hall, and Irene's Palace of Cosmetology.

5. The word *raze* means to destroy or to level.

6. The two rewards the white slave owner promised the slave for completing the chores were freedom and a parcel of land.

7. The hilly land where the black people lived was the Bottom.

8. The hilly land got its name because the slave owner said that the land was the bottom of Heaven.

9. The little girl introduced in the chapter and who grew into a woman in the Bottom is Sula.

10. The white people eventually viewed the hilly land as attractive.

Suggested Essay Topics

1. Part One stimulates the reader to continue the book by leaving the reader with some unresolved issues. What are three of the unresolved questions at the end of the chapter? Describe each.

2. Change is a major theme in this chapter. Cite and describe at least four instances of change in the chapter.

Chapter One: 1919

New Characters:

Shadrack: *a young man with a psychological war injury from World War I; founder of National Suicide Day*

Male nurse: *the balding man who treats Shadrack in the hospital*

Reverend Deal: *a minister of the Bottom who accepts National Suicide Day*

Summary

Every January 3rd after 1920, Shadrack celebrated National Suicide Day. For many years, he was the only one to celebrate. The events of 1917 resulted in his establishment of the holiday.

During World War I, Shadrack, who was barely 20, and his comrades met the enemy on a French field in December of 1917. After seeing his friend killed, Shadrack awoke in a hospital. Even though Shadrack was still hallucinating and violent, the hospital discharged him with $217, his papers, and a full suit of clothes.

Upon his arrival in town, Shadrack's hallucinations continued. When the police locked him in jail for vagrancy and intoxication, the 22-year-old felt relieved.

After the police officers read Shadrack's hospital discharge papers with his personal information on them, they returned him to the Bottom on the back of a truck. For 12 days Shadrack struggled to order his thoughts.

On January 3, 1920, Shadrack walked down Carpenter's Road with a cowbell and a hangman's rope. The people were wary but listened to what Shadrack had to say. He announced on the Charter National Suicide Day in 1920 that this was the only chance for a year for residents to kill others or themselves. Gradually the annual event became a part of the neighborhood.

Analysis

Morrison uses a limited omniscient style when she takes the reader into the mind of only one character: Shadrack. Her descriptions of Shadrack's thoughts and feelings enable the reader to see the world through Shadrack's eyes (Menippean satire). For instance, the narrator describes how Shadrack saw through his tears his own fingers. His fingers seemed to fuse with the fabric of his laces and to move in and out of the eyelets of his shoes.

Morrison also presents the character to the reader through Shadrack's actions; through the narrator the reader learns that Shadrack sold fish two days a week and "...the rest of the week he was drunk, loud, obscene, funny, and outrageous."

The reactions of others to Shadrack also reveal his character; for instance, the reader finds that hospital workers bind Shadrack into a straitjacket. Additional information shows the reactions of others to Shadrack after his return from war:

> "At first the people in the town were frightened; they knew
> Shadrack was crazy, but that did not mean that he didn't have
> any sense or, even more important, that he had no power."

The way that others speak to Shadrack shows how they view him; for example, the nurse has no sympathy for Shadrack and asks, "'Private? We're not going to have any trouble today, are we? Are we, Private?'"

Shadrack is a dynamic character: one who changes. He is a young boy who enters World War I. When he returns, he is damaged severely from the action on the field in France. Shadrack is also a round character that the reader knows well. After reading the chapter, one knows what Shadrack thinks and feels. For example, "...With extreme care he lifted one arm and was relieved to find his hand attached to his wrist." One also learns how Shadrack

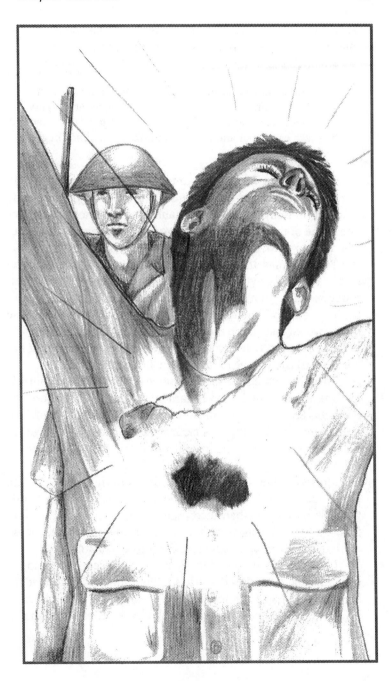

reacts to others; for instance, the reader finds that Shadrack "never touched anybody, never fought, never caressed."

Shadrack's appearance also helps reveal him to the reader:

> "The sheriff looked through the bars at the young man with the matted hair. He had read through his prisoner's papers and hailed a farmer....In the back of the wagon, supported by sacks of squash and hills of pumpkins, Shadrack began a struggle...."

There is symbolism in the name of the road (Carpenter's Road). Shadrack walks down Carpenter's Road when he tries to bring order for himself and others by establishing National Suicide Day. The name of the road reminds the reader of an earlier carpenter who walked down a road before his crucifixion.

The integral setting helps both to illuminate Shadrack to the reader and to clarify the conflicts which are to come. Many communities do not have the social relationships that the people in the hills develop. The story would not work in such a place because others would just ignore the actions of a character like Shadrack. Perhaps the tight-knit town to which Morrison returned after her failed marriage was the model for the Bottom.

There is symbolism also in the name of the character Shadrack. Like the Shadrack in the Old Testament who survived the fiery furnace, this Shadrack, too, withstands his own test of fire. Morrison even notes that the minister acknowledges Shadrack's walk down Carpenter's Road and incorporates the event into his own life and sermon.

Morrison shows how innocent the Bottom people are. She shows them readily accepting others and even what life hands them. She also shows them incorporating National Suicide Day into their thoughts, behavior, and lives. Their image perpetuates the myth of the docile slave begun in the introductory chapter.

Morrison makes use of many literary devices. Alliteration is evident when she writes that "He shuffled, grew dizzy, stopped for breath, started again, stumbling and sweating... ." A metaphor is evident when Morrison notes that Shadrack "...let his mind slip

into whatever cave mouths of memory it chose." An example of personification is obvious when Morrison indicates that "...the blackness greeted him... ."

Study Questions

1. What event did Shadrack establish?

2. In what year did Shadrack receive his discharge from the hospital?

3. What did Shadrack feel the first time he encountered shellfire?

4. What were the two possible reasons that the hospital discharged Shadrack?

5. What were the charges the police listed for arresting Shadrack?

6. What road did Shadrack march down annually?

7. What two things did Shadrack carry on his trip down Carpenter's Road?

8. In what year did Shadrack establish the national holiday?

9. What appeal did he give to the people of the Bottom each January 3rd?

10. What was the reasoning behind Shadrack's establishment of National Suicide Day?

Answers

1. Shadrack established National Suicide Day.

2. Shadrack received his discharge from the hospital in 1919.

3. Shadrack felt only a tack in his shoe the first time he encountered shellfire.

4. The hospital discharged Shadrack because of his violence or another priority, such as the limited number of beds in the hospital.

5. The charges the police listed for arresting Shadrack were vagrancy and intoxication.

6. Shadrack marched down Carpenter's Road annually.

7. Shadrack carried a hangman's rope and a cow's bell on his trip down Carpenter's Road.

8. Shadrack established the national holiday in 1920.

9. Each January 3rd, Shadrack told the people this was their only chance to kill others or themselves.

10. The reasoning behind Shadrack's establishment of National Suicide Day was to establish order because Shadrack was afraid of the unexpected.

Suggested Essay Topics

1. A common saying is that if one is silent, that person assents. Do you see any examples of assenting silence in this chapter?

2. Describe Shadrack's relationships with others in the community on days other than National Suicide Day.

Chapter Two: 1920

New Characters:

Cecile: *great aunt to Wiley Wright and grandmother to Helene; took Helene from the Sundown House and reared her in New Orleans*

Helene Sabat: *daughter of a Creole prostitute; born behind the red shutters of Sundown House*

Wiley Wright: *nephew of Cecile; resided in Medallion, Ohio; married Helene Sabat, when she was 16; a seaman in port only three days out of every 16; served as cook aboard the ship*

Nel: *the daughter of Helene and Wiley after their ninth year of marriage*

Henri Martin: *New Orleans resident who writes to Helene to tell her of her grandmother's illness*

Porter: *the colored man who points Helene and Nel to the coach*

Conductor: *the white man who calls Helene "gal" and who questions Helene's and Nel's presence in the white section of the coach*

Black woman and her four children: *passengers who boarded in Tuscaloosa; the woman shows Helene and Nel the field that is used for a restroom*

Rochelle: *Helene's mother and Nel's grandmother*

Eva: *Sula's grandmother*

Hannah: *Sula's mother; Eva's oldest child*

Summary

Helene Sabat was born in Sundown House in New Orleans; her mother was a prostitute. Her grandmother Cecile took the child to rear. Young Helene married Wiley Wright and returned with him to Medallion, Ohio. Wiley was a seaman who was home only three days out of every 16. His job aboard the ship was to cook. After nine years, Wiley and Helene had a baby girl, whom they named Nel.

Helene received a letter from Henri Martin. The letter said that Cecile was sick. Armed with her manner, her bearing, and a new dress, Helene decided to return to New Orleans. She and her daughter traveled by train in November of 1920.

On the train they made a mistake and entered the wrong car. The conductor talked demeaningly at the pair, and Helene did the unthinkable: she smiled! The smile brought the contempt of all the black men in the car. Nel saw her mother turn to custard. Nel resolved never to bring this look on herself.

The trip south took two days. Helene and Nel left behind the areas where the restrooms were marked "White" and "Colored" and entered an area where the restroom for them was just a field of grass.

Helene and Nel arrived too late to see Cecile; Cecile had died shortly before their arrival. Nel met Rochelle, Helene's mother. Nel made a discovery on this trip—her first and last from Medallion. Nel found that she was her own person- independent of anyone else.

Nel formed a bond of friendship with Sula. Each preferred the home of the other. Nel's mother manipulated others and kept her home oppressively neat. Sula's home was quite different;

her mother, Hannah, never scolded or manipulated. Guests were frequent in Sula's home and dirty dishes remained in the sink. Eva, Sula's one-legged grandmother, read dreams to the girls and gave them peanuts from her pockets.

Analysis

This chapter is rich with contrasts; the author uses antiphonal characteristics to make the characters and settings more vivid. Morrison describes the contrasting homes and families of Sula and Nel in detail. Medallion and New Orleans were unlike in many ways; Morrison notes some of these differences. Nel discovers marked contrasts as the train approaches the South.

Diction is an important part of constructing the characters for the reader. Morrison records Rochelle's Creole carefully for the reader: "'I don't know what happen to de house. Long time paid for. You be think' on it? Oui?'" The words of the black woman who had boarded the train in Tuscaloosa reflect the speech of the South: "Yonder" and "We be pullin' in direc'lin."

Morrison takes the reader inside the mind of Nel and allows the reader to view the happenings through Nel's perspective. The reader finds that Nel sees her mother as "custard" after the encounter with the conductor and dislikes what she observes. Nel even takes some satisfaction in the discomfort of her mother in the presence of the conductor and the men in the train car.

Identity is an important theme in this chapter. Young Nel begins to establish an identity of who she is. After her return to Medallion, Nel says, "'I'm me. I'm not their daughter. I'm not Nel. I'm me. Me.'" Nel's attitude is similar to Morrison's; Toni Morrison admits that she does not allow others to control her feelings toward herself.

Morrison continues to use stylistic devices. For example, a metaphor is evident when Nel calls Rochelle a "painted canary." Descriptive passages help the reader to visualize the sights that Nel sees; one example is when Morrison notes "...the muddy eyes of the men who stood like wrecked Dorics... ."

The imagery that Morrison uses when she describes Sula's house allows the reader to experience the sights, sounds, and feelings of a visitor:

"...As for Nel, she preferred Sula's woolly house, where a pot of something was always cooking on the stove; where the mother, Hannah, never scolded or gave directions; where all sorts of people dropped in; where newspapers were stacked in the hallway, and dirty dishes left for hours at a time in the sink, and where a one-legged grandmother named Eva handed you goobers from deep inside her pockets or read you a dream."

Sula describes the friendship of two women. Such a story was unusual in its day. The theme of women's friendship was a topic not generally treated in the 1970s.

Study Questions

1. Where did Wiley Wright live?

2. Whom did Wiley Wright marry?

3. What was Wiley Wright's daughter's name?

4. In what city was Helene born?

5. Who was Helene's mother?

6. In what house was Helene born?

7. How did Helene and Nel know that they were too late to see Cecile alive?

8. What was Helene's reaction when the conductor spoke disparagingly to her?

9. Which of the discoveries that Nel made on her trip to New Orleans was most important?

10. Who was Nel's friend?

Answers

1. Wiley Wright lived in Medallion, Ohio.

2. Wiley Wright married Helene.

3. Nel was Wiley Wright's daughter.

4. Helene was born in New Orleans.

5. Helene's mother was Rochelle.

6. Helene was born in Sundown House.

7. Helene and Nel knew that they were too late to see Cecile alive when they saw the black crepe wreath with the purple ribbon.

8. When the conductor spoke disparagingly to Helene, Helene smiled, and that brought her the contempt of the black men in the train car.

9. The most important discovery that Nel made on her trip to New Orleans was that she was herself, not her parents or anyone else.

10. Nel's friend was Sula.

Suggested Essay Topics

1. When Nel said that her grandmother's skin was soft, Helene made a comment. What was the comment? What do you think Helene meant by the comment? Can you think of instances in which this might be a good analogy?

2. Compare and contrast the homes and families of Sula and Nel.

Chapter Three: 1921

New Characters:

BoyBoy: *Eva's husband and Sula's grandfather*

Pearl: *Eva's daughter; real name is Eva; younger than Hannah; aunt of Sula; married at 14 and moved to Flint, Michigan*

Plum: *Eva's son; real name is Ralph*

Suggs family: *gave food to Eva and her children; gave castor oil to Eva when Plum was constipated; poured water on Hannah when fire consumed her*

Mr. and Mrs. Jackson: *gave milk to Eva and her children*

Eva's adopted children: *all three named dewey; one with red hair and freckles, one half-Mexican, one deeply black; no individuality of mind*

Rekus: *husband of Hannah; father of Sula; died when Sula was three*

Tar Baby: *along with the deweys, first to follow Shadrack; came in 1920; had some—or all—white blood; mountain boy; alcoholic*

Mrs. Reed: *teacher; gave all three deweys the last name of King and the same age*

Buckland Reed: *husband of the teacher, Mrs. Reed; takes numbers from the residents of the Bottom; makes a comment about Eva's leg being worth $10,000*

Summary

Sula Peace lived in a house built to the specifications of her grandmother, Eva Peace. Eva was the African-American owner who added to the house over a five-year period. Her whims and requirements changed during this time. Some rooms had three doors; others, only one. Some rooms opened onto porches; some had no entrances from the inside.

Eva's husband was BoyBoy. They had three children: Hannah, Eva (also known as Pearl), and Ralph (also called Plum). BoyBoy did what he liked: womanize, abuse Eva, and drink. He left Eva after five years of marriage; she had only five eggs, $1.65, three children, and three beets.

Eva depended on neighbors like the Suggs family and the Jacksons for food and milk. One night after helping Plum end a bout of severe constipation, Eva left the children with the Suggs family "for a day." Eighteen months later she came back with one leg, two crutches, a new pocketbook, and fanciful tales about the loss of her leg. Eva gave Mrs. Suggs $10.00 and began building a house near the cabin where she and BoyBoy had lived. She rented the cabin which now had an outhouse, although it did not have one for the first year she and BoyBoy had occupied it.

BoyBoy returned to visit when Plum was three. Uncertain of her emotions, Eva served BoyBoy lemonade. They talked politely

for a while until he, with his smell of money and new clothes, returned to his city woman who waited for him under the pear tree.
Eva now felt toward BoyBoy only one emotion: hate. She began to
retreat to her room and left only once after the year 1910. On that
occasion Eva started a fire, the smell of which remained in her hair
for months.

In 1921, Eva took in three children she saw from the balcony.
She named all three dewey. The three deweys were inseparable.
She also took in a man she called Tar Baby. He was interested only
in drink. He and the three deweys eventually became the first to
join Shadrack in the celebration of National Suicide Day.

Like their mother, the Peace women loved men. Pearl married at 14 and moved to Flint, Michigan. Hannah married Rekus,
who fathered Sula. Rekus died when Sula was three. Sula is aware
of the fact that her mother begins to entertain men in their home;
she sees her mother enter the pantry with men. From Hannah, Sula
learns that sex is pleasant, frequent, and unremarkable.

Eva's last child was Ralph, or Plum. Plum went to war in 1917.
When he returned in 1919, he did not come directly home. He spoke
little, slept a lot, stole from his family, and became very thin.
Hannah found a bent spoon which was black from cooking (a sign
of drug abuse).

One night, Eva went to Plum's room, gathered Plum in her
arms, and rocked him. She got some items from the kitchen and
returned to his room. She doused him with kerosene and set him
on fire.

Analysis

Conflict is the distinguishing feature of this chapter. It is the
desire for resolution of conflict in the plot that keeps the reader
attentive to *Sula*. There are many types of conflict in "1921."

A recurring conflict in "1921," and in the entire book, is that
between individualism and conformity. Eva tries to make the
adopted children she called dewey alike; even the teacher, the narrator admits, cannot tell the children apart even though they are
quite different in appearance. The children, however, are noncon-
formists and try to resist the molds imposed upon them. They join
with another who is an individual: Shadrack.

Another conflict apparent in "1921" and in the book as a whole is the conflict between good and evil. The reader wants to know if evil or good brought about Plum's death. The reader wants to know if one will triumph over the other in the book and in the lives of the people of the Bottom.

The character Hannah experiences a different type of conflict. Hannah has a conflict with society. Because of her "loose" lifestyle, Hannah makes many enemies in the community. Morrison explains that the "good" women object to her activities; the prostitutes object to the free trade Hannah gives; and the other women object to her liaisons without love or emotion.

Conflict between characters is an integral part of "1921." The reader finds out about the conflicts between Eva and BoyBoy and between Eva and Plum. Conflict between person and self is also evident when Eva must make the decision to leave her family and to burn her son to death. Fire figures prominently in *Sula*, as it did in Morrison's life.

Morrison weaves the theme of love throughout the chapter. The love objects and acts of love vary. Hannah has sex with the men in the Bottom for pleasure—not love. Plum exhibits love—for drugs. Tar Baby also loves wine. BoyBoy loves three things: drink, women, and abusing Eva.

The theme of good versus evil began with the contrasting of the Bottom and the valley and continues when the characters perform evil and disheartening acts: stealing from family, ignoring others and their needs, and setting fire to a family member—although Eva professed to have done this in love.

Throughout the novel Eva equates her love for others with responsibility. This constant expression of responsibility makes Eva a static character. Eva expresses love for her dynamic (changing) son Plum through her "responsible actions." She must make sure that Plum succeeds as a man because she loves him. This love and the resulting responsibility make it necessary for Eva to burn her son to death.

A strong feature of the chapter and of Morrison's writing is her effective characterization. Morrison reveals many dimensions of the round, important characters to make them real to the reader. An analysis of Morrison's methods of characterization shows that her techniques vary from one character in *Sula* to another. For

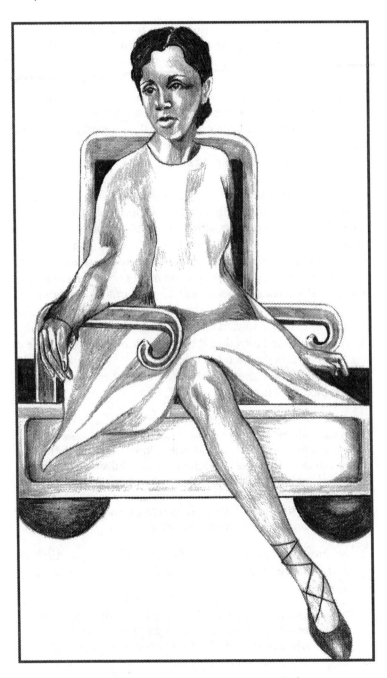

instance, Morrison uses many different techniques with the piv-
otal character of Eva Peace. The reader is able to see Eva through
many eyes and through many devices. For example, Morrison calls
Eva Peace the "creator and sovereign"; this is an example of the
narrator/writer giving the reader an opinion. The writer shows Eva
in action to help reveal her completely; for instance, the reader
finds Eva sitting "in a wagon on the third floor directing the lives of
her children, friends, strays, and a constant stream of boarders."
Eva is proactive as she takes in children and retreats to her bedroom.

The narrator inserts words which give the reader information
about Eva Peace. This static character expresses her love for others—even visiting children—through her responsible actions; for
instance, she is the perfect hostess when "...she began some fear-
ful story about it [her missing leg]—generally to entertain children."

The reader finds that Eva's diction makes her a real person; for
instance, she responds, upon hearing of Plum's dying moments,
"'Is? My baby? Burning?'" Another means of characterization are
the actions of others toward Eva; for example, the readers find that
"Unless Eva herself introduced the subject, no one ever spoke of
her disability; they pretended to ignore it... ." Eva's physical description and the impression she makes on others help to round
out the picture of her:

> "...the remaining one [leg] was magnificent...Her dresses
> were mid-calf so that her one glamorous leg was always in
> view...[Her] wagon was so low that children who spoke to her
> standing up were eye level with her, and adults, standing or
> sitting, had to look down at her...But they didn't know it. They
> had the impression that they were looking up at her, up into
> the open distances of her eyes, up into the soft black of her
> nostrils and up at the crest of her chin."

An important part of the chapter is the setting, particularly
the house where Sula lived. The description of the house itself
is graphic.

> "Sula Peace lived in a house of many rooms that had been
> built over a period of five years to the specifications of its
> owner, who kept on adding things: more stairways—there

were three sets to the second floor—more rooms, doors and stoops. There were rooms that had three doors, others that opened out on the porch only and were inaccessible from any other part of the house; others that you could get to only by going through somebody's bedroom... ."

The creator and sovereign in this house lives at the highest level: the third floor—which signifies Heaven and the supreme location. The others in the family are in the nether regions.

The time frame for "1921" does not adhere to a strictly chronological arrangement. There are flashbacks; for instance, the narrator takes the reader back in time to the construction of the Peace home, ahead to the time of the troubled marriage of BoyBoy and Eva, and ahead to the year 1921 when Eva burns Plum.

Morrison uses many stylistic devices in "1921" to make the action, the characters, and the setting real to the reader. She uses the onomatopoeic word "whoosh" to describe the sound of the flames as they engulf Plum. The diction that Morrison very carefully records is another important stylistic device. For example, Eva says, "'Tell them deweys to cut out that noise.'" Connotation helps the reader draw a picture of Tar Baby; Morrison describes his "milky skin and cornsilk hair." Through the use of a simile, the reader can feel the emotions of Eva when BoyBoy comes to visit:

"...It hit her like a sledge hammer, and it was then that she knew what to feel. A liquid trail of hate flooded her chest."

Imagery is an important part of the chapter. Morrison writes:

"...Eva squatted there wondering why she had come all the way out there to free his stools, and what was she doing down on her haunches with her beloved baby boy warmed by her body in the almost total darkness, her shins and teeth freezing, her nostrils assailed."

There is foreshadowing, another stylistic device, in the chapter. The reader suspects that when Sula learns that sex is pleasant, frequent, and unremarkable, she will follow in the footsteps of her mother.

It becomes evident to the reader, particularly in "1921," that *Sula* is a tragedy. It seems doubtful that all the conflicts can be

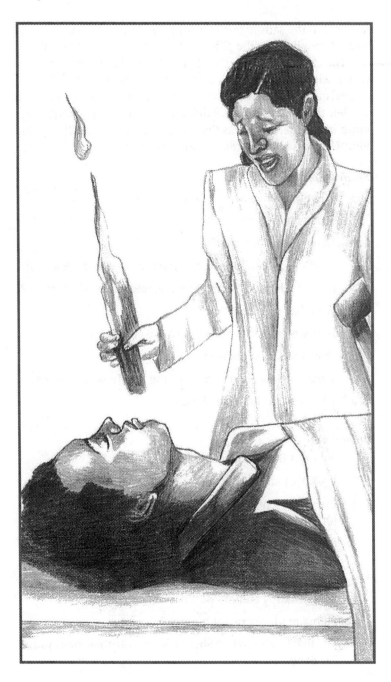

resolved to the satisfaction of the reader. Further tragic develop-
ments seem likely as the plot unfolds.

The chapter is not a closed one. The author again leaves the
reader with a desire to read more because there are many unanswered questions: How did Eva lose her leg? Where did Eva go when
she left the children? Where did Eva get the money to build the
rambling house? What was the result of the fire? Why did Eva kill
Plum? The reader must read another chapter!

Study Questions

1. What was Sula's relationship to Eva?
2. Who was Eva's husband?
3. Name Eva's three children.
4. How was Eva different when she returned to the Bottom?
5. How was Plum different when he returned to the Bottom?
6. What happened to Plum?
7. Who were the first people to join Shadrack?
8. Why did Hannah make love during the day?
9. What did Sula learn about making love from her mother?
10. What was Tar Baby's bad habit?

Answers

1. Sula was Eva's granddaughter.
2. Eva's husband was BoyBoy.
3. Eva's three children are Hannah, Plum (or Ralph), and Eva
   (or Pearl).
4. Eva was different when she returned to the Bottom because
   she was missing a leg.
5. Plum was different when he returned to the Bottom because
   he was a drug addict.
6. Plum's mother, Eva, set him on fire.
7. The first people to join Shadrack were the three deweys and
   Tar Baby.

8. Hannah made love during the day because sleeping with someone was a commitment and an act of trust.

9. Sula learned from her mother that making love was pleasant, unremarkable, and a frequent occurrence.

10. Tar Baby's bad habit was drinking wine.

Suggested Essay Topics

1. Describe as completely as possible the house built over a five-year period by an owner whose specifications continued to change. Now, add your description of some other unusual features the house might have had.

2. Change is a frequent feature of this chapter. Which characters seem to be dynamic, or changing, characters? Are there characters in this chapter who are static, or nonchanging? Explain your answer.

Chapter Four: 1922

New Characters:

Ajax: *21-year-old man with sinister beauty; a frequenter of the pool halls; calls Sula "pig meat" when he sees her; Sula's lover*

Chicken Little: *a little boy whom Sula swings around; drowns when he slips from Sula's hands and goes into the lake*

Patsy and Valentine: *Hannah's two friends who are visiting with her the day Chicken Little drowned*

Four white, Irish boys: *newly arrived residents of the Bottom; taunted the girls*

Bargeman: *the one who found Chicken Little's body*

Summary

The men in the community of the Bottom had a frequent haunt to watch girls and women pass. They squatted on Carpenter's Road,

the four blocks of businesses in the neighborhood. The old men were now kind and remembered the days past; they often tipped their hats. The young men opened and closed their thighs. All stared at the girls and women as they passed.

Ajax was one of the young men who frequented the area and hurled epithets. Often the words he used were harmless, but his way of saying them gave him a reputation of having a foul mouth. When Nel and Sula deliberately pass these boys and men on the excuse of wanting to get ice cream—which it was really too cool to enjoy—Ajax called out the words, "pig meat." The two 12-year-olds were delighted.

Four Irish boys often followed the girls from school and even tried to pass them from hand to hand, tear their clothes, and do anything else they were able to do to harass them. Sula, with her birthmark that looked like a long-stemmed rose, and Nel, with her developing body, usually avoided the path the boys might take. One day, however, Sula persuaded Nel to take the shortest way home with her. When the boys began to follow them, Sula cut off the tip of her finger in order to show the boys her lack of fear and what she could do to them.

Nel's mother wanted her daughter to be attractive. Each Saturday she had Nel use the hot comb. Each night she sent Nel to bed with a clothespin on her nose. Nel began to slip the pin under the cover each night after she met Sula.

One hot summer day the girls decided to follow the boys to the lake. Sula slipped back into her house to use the bathroom and heard her mother say that she did not like her daughter even though she loved her. Sula was very upset, but she did not tell Nel what she heard.

When the girls arrived at the lake, they dug two holes and put in glass, rocks, leaves, and other debris. They climbed a tree with Chicken Little. Sula took him by his arms and swung him around; Chicken Little slipped from her arms, flew into the lake, and drowned.

Sula was afraid that someone had seen. She ran to see if Shadrack could have observed what happened. She found Shadrack's cabin. When he surprised her, she turned to ask him a question. He, however, answered a question she had never asked. His answer was, "Always."

Nel assured Sula that she had not meant to drown Chicken. Nel said that it was not Sula's fault. Nel was also very concerned because Sula had lost her belt.

Because of the unimportance the white men placed on the child's dead body and his family's feelings, it was three days before the family received Chicken's body. At the funeral, the girls appeared deeply moved. The women acknowledged that the only way to escape the hand of God was to get in it. The girls held each other's hands tightly. Gradually their hand clasp loosened, and they appeared like any other young girls.

Analysis

Morrison makes use of many stylistic devices in this chapter. When Sula enters Shadrack's cabin, Morrison uses personification: "...heard the hinges weep." She uses imagery, for instance, when she describes Nel and Sula as "wishbone thin." Dialect is evident as Chicken says "I'm a tell my brovver." She uses alliteration when she writes "the neatness, the order startled her, but more surprising was the restfulness." A metaphor is evident when the writer describes Nel and Sula walking through a "valley of eyes." Morrison uses contrasts to describe the street, or valley of eyes, even further; she describes the road as being "...chilled by the wind and heated by the embarrassment of appraising stares." A simile is used to describe the two girls as being "like tightrope walkers." Imagery is a descriptive technique used to describe the weather: "A summer limp with the weight of blossomed things." Morrison makes an allusion to the Bible and the Biblical character Ham.

In this chapter, Morrison frequently uses the stylistic device of connotation; that is, she does not say exactly what she means. Instead she makes a reference to something else to create the feeling she wants the reader to have. For example, Morrison refers to "the smell of hot tar"; to comprehend the expression, one would have to have experienced the smell.

The themes of loneliness and sexism are important parts of "1922." Morrison discusses the loneliness of the two girls before their friendship began. She describes the sexual harassment of the men as they stare at the women and girls walking past. She refers to sexism again when she states that Sula and Nel "…were neither white nor male, and that all freedom and triumph was forbidden to them…" She experienced sexual and racial harassment in her own life.

Racism is an important theme in "1922" and figures prominently into the incidents surrounding the death of Chicken Little. A white bargeman finds the body that afternoon, but it is too much trouble for him, the ferryman, or the sheriff to inform the family. It is three days before the family receives the body.

Morrison allows the reader to enter the mind of the white bargeman to show his ugly, hate-filled, racist thoughts. The bargeman immediately assumes that Chicken Little's own parents have drowned the child. The reader finds that the bargeman regards the African-Americans as nothing "…but animals, fit for nothing but substitutes for mules, only mules didn't kill each other the way niggers did."

The sheriff and the bargeman speak openly and voice their racist attitudes. The sheriff asks why the bargeman did not just throw the body back in the water. The bargeman admits he should have never taken it out in the first place. At last, the ferryman agrees to take the body back in the morning—not at once.

The reader is also aware, through Morrison's writing, of the racism in the community of Medallion—there is discrimination as well as reverse discrimination. For instance, the reader finds that when some Irish move into the area, they encounter:

> "…a strange accent, a pervasive fear of their religion and firm resistance to their attempts to find work.….In part their place in this world was secured only when they echoed the old residents' attitude toward blacks."

Morrison gives a hint of the events to come with her foreshadowing. She writes that "The birthmark was to grow darker as the years passed, but now it was the same shade as her gold-flecked eyes, which, to the end, were as steady and clean as rain." (This birthmark and water or rain are to figure prominently throughout the book.) On the same page Morrison mentions that there was a time when Sula would retain a mood for weeks in defense of her friend Nel. Another example of foreshadowing—this time a hint of Chicken Little's death—occurs when the girls dig and fill a grave.

The words "saw" and "watch" are important words in the chapter. The men *watched* the women and girls walk past them; the word "watched" implies they deliberately stopped. Sula is afraid that someone *saw* Chicken Little drown; the word "saw" indicates that one caught a glimpse of something—perhaps unintentionally. The words will surface again later in the book.

There is a parallel between Shadrack and Sula in the chapter. Both appear not to be afraid of death or pain, but they both seem to fear the uncertainty of when it may come. Like Shadrack, Sula tries to gain control over the conditions and seeks to force the boys into showing their hand when she has control of the situation.

It is significant that the boys drop all pretense of innocence when Sula shows them the knife. This theme of innocence has already surfaced in the introduction when the slave owner dupes the (innocent) slave into taking the hill land.

Morrison reveals more of the character of Shadrack through "1922." The surroundings of Shadrack tell the reader about the character:

> "...The neatness, the order startled her, but more surprising was the restfulness. Everything was so tiny, so common, so unthreatening... .This cottage? This sweet old cottage? With its made-up bed? With its rag rug and wooden table? Sula stood in the middle of the little room..."

Physical features—the hands of Shadrack—and their movements when Sula goes to his cottage divulge a side of Shadrack the reader has not seen before:

> "...she saw his hand resting upon the door frame. His fingers, barely touching the wood, were arranged in a graceful arc. Relieved and encouraged (no one with hands like that, no one with fingers curved around wood so tenderly could kill her)..."

Shadrack's words and his facial expressions when he speaks give Sula and the reader information about this person:

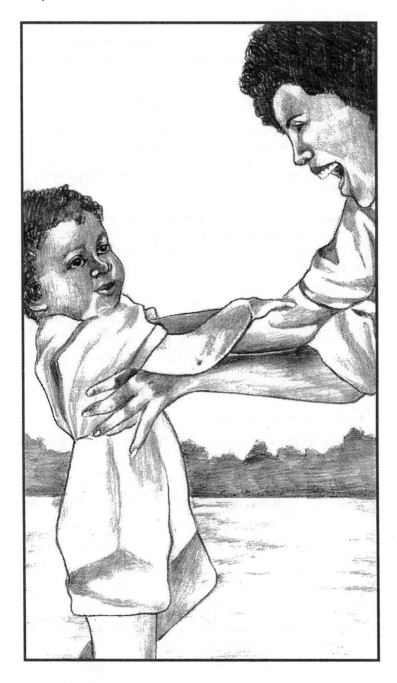

"He was smiling, a great smile, heavy with lust and time to come. He nodded his head as though answering a question, and said in a pleasant conversational tone, a tone of cooled butter, 'Always.'"

The narrator adds to Shadrack's character revelation in "1922."

"...The terrible Shad who walked about with his penis out, who peed in front of ladies and girl-children, the only black who could curse white people and get away with it, who drank in the road from the mouth of the bottle, who shouted and shook in the streets..."

Again, the author makes the reader continue to read. Also, Morrison once more leaves the reader with many unsettled questions. What happened to the belt? Will the sheriff find out about Sula's crime? Has Shadrack really been watching them?

Study Questions

1. What did Nel's mother want Nel to do to make her nose attractive?

2. How did Sula convince the boys that she was not afraid of them and could take care of herself?

3. What disturbing thing did Sula hear her mother say?

4. How did Chicken Little die?

5. How long was it before the family of Chicken Little received his body?

6. Who found the body of Chicken Little?

7. What answer did Shadrack make to the unasked question?

8. What did Sula lose when Chicken Little died?

9. What does Morrison say happens to a handclasp?

10. What did Nel say about Sula's part in the accident?

Answers

1. Nel's mother wants Nel to sleep with a clothespin on her nose to make her nose more attractive.

2. Sula convinced the boys she was not afraid of them by showing them a knife and cutting off the tip of her own finger.

3. Sula heard her mother say she loved but did not like her daughter.

4. Chicken Little drowned when his body flew from Sula's grasp while she was swinging him near the water.

5. It was three days before the family of Chicken Little received his body.

6. The bargeman found the body of Chicken Little.

7. Shadrack's answer to the unasked question was, "Always."

8. Sula lost her belt when Chicken Little died.

9. Morrison said a handclasp would stay above ground forever.

10. Nel told Sula that it was not Sula's fault.

Suggested Essay Topics

1. Morrison writes that Nel and Sula stood away from the grave after the service.

   "...They held hands and knew that only the coffin would lie in the earth; the bubbly laughter and the press of fingers in the palm would stay aboveground forever."

   What do you think she meant by this passage? Explain your answer fully.

2. Morrison mentions the most dreadful pain that there is. What does she say that this pain is? Explain what she means.

Chapter Five: 1923

New Characters:

Iceman: *delivers ice to the homes*

Willy Fields: *orderly who saved Eva from bleeding to death and received her curse for doing so the rest of her life*

Summary

In this chapter, the second strange thing happens; Hannah brought a peck of Kentucky Wonders into Eva's room and asked if Eva ever loved her children.

Eva reprimanded her daughter for wondering and reminded Hannah that there was no playing in 1895. Eva began to reflect on an earlier time. She remembered her husband leaving her, Plum's constipation, and the three beets which were all she had when her husband left. Eva remarked that Hannah would have been dead if Eva had not loved her.

Hannah asked a second question: why had Eva burned Plum? Eva explained to Hannah that she burned Plum because he tried to return to her womb through his drugs and because she wanted him to die like a man.

The wind was the first strange thing that happened that day. The people welcomed the wind, however, because they thought that it meant rain.

Hannah lay down for a while after washing the beans and dreamed of a wedding in a red dress. She mentioned this dream to her mother at breakfast; she had brought her mother scrambled eggs without the whites to bring them good luck on their number choice. Neither she nor her mother bothered to look the dream number up because they both knew the dream number was 522. Eva said she would place bets on that number when Mr. Buckland Reed came. This was the third strange thing.

Hannah went into the yard and kneeled to light the yard fire for canning. Eva watched her from her window. When Eva returned to the window after searching for her lost comb, she saw that Hannah was on fire; this strange thing was the fourth strange

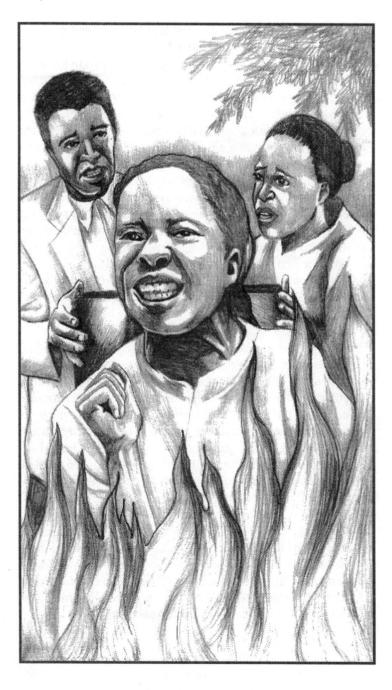

happening—or fifth, depending on whether the reader counts Sula's craziness in watching Hannah burn.

Eva threw herself through the window and tried to place her own body over the flaming body of Hannah. Hannah moved about in the flame, and Eva could not reach her in time. Mr. and Mrs. Suggs poured the tub of hot water, with the tomatoes still in it, on Hannah. It was too late. Hannah died—probably on the way to the hospital with her bleeding mother beside her in the ambulance.

Eva would have bled to death at the hospital had it not been for the orderly Willy Fields. Everyone seemed to have forgotten Eva, and Willy reminded them that there was another patient there. Eva, however, was not grateful for the rescue and cursed Willy every day for 37 years until she was 90; Eva would have cursed him longer, but she became forgetful.

Eva decided the red in the dream Hannah had before her death symbolized fire and that the wedding meant death. She also recalled and told others that she had seen Sula looking as Hannah burned.

Analysis

Morrison entices the reader to continue reading from the first sentence of the chapter. Morrison mentions "the second strange thing that happened." The sentence makes the reader want to read on and to find out about the *first* strange thing which happened. This sequence keeps one turning the pages. To cause even further curiosity in the reader, in the same sentence is a reference to Kentucky Wonders; most readers will not know what these are. There is, therefore, at least one problem with no immediate solution to keep the reader engaged in reading *Sula* for a while longer.

The chapter is not in chronological order. There are flashbacks, a stylistic device that Morrison employs frequently. For instance, Eva reflects on an earlier time when she sat in the cold outhouse with the baby, Plum. Morrison also uses foreshadowing—a glimpse into or a hint about the future. She tells the reader that Eva lives a long time. The chapter title "1923," then, is not a chronological chapter as its title might lead one to suspect.

Morrison makes use of imagery to give the reader a clear picture of the action of finding Eva after Hannah's burning. For instance, she writes:

> "...They found her on her stomach by the forsythia bushes calling Hannah's name and dragging her body through the sweet peas and clover that grew under the forsythia by the side of the house...The blood from her face cuts filled her eyes so she could not see, could only smell the familiar odor of cooked flesh."

The writer goes into the minds of several characters, primarily Eva and Hannah. Eva reveals that Sula is interested in watching her mother burn. The reader, however, still wonders why Sula watched Hannah burn without helping; this means that the chapter is an open-ended one that keeps the reader interested and ensures that the reading continues.

Morrison makes use of many stylistic devices. For instance, she uses similes. An example of one of these descriptive phrases using *like* is "...gesturing and bobbing like a sprung jack-in-the-box." Morrison's careful renditions of the characters' diction give the reader a flavor of the time. For instance, Eva says, "'Give me that again. Flat out to fit my head.'"

Morrison's own grandmother made use of dream books; Morrison's knowledge of this technique and of superstitions affects the content of the chapter. In "1922," Hannah has a dream about a red dress and a wedding; both Hannah and Eva know the dream book well enough to know the number for that dream is 522. They plan to use that number for placing their bets when Mr. Buckland Reed comes; this reminds the reader of Morrison's grandmother. To help ensure their good luck, Hannah brings Eva scrambled eggs with the whites left out. Sula is 13 (unlucky); this is a time when she is an adolescent and no longer a child and when she loses her mother to fire. These references indicate the writer's own knowledge of superstitions.

Morrison uses irony after this incident. The good luck they had hoped for turns into bad luck. Hannah burns to death and Eva is almost killed trying to save her daughter. Symbolism plays a part in the incident. From her hospital ward Eva remembers that weddings mean death and the red wedding gown symbolizes the fire; Morrison again weaves her knowledge of superstition and family heritage into the writing. The cool ice in the beginning of the chapter turns to fire.

An important theme in the chapter is love. Hannah begins by asking Eva if she loved Hannah, Pearl, and Plum. Eva equates responsibility with love in her answer. When Hannah asks why Eva burned Plum, Eva explains that Plum tried to return to his mother's womb and that she made sure he behaved as a man; she was, in effect, exercising responsibility through setting fire to Plum because of her love for him. Sula, on the other hand, does not indicate her love for her mother by exercising responsibility for her mother's well-being. Neither did she take the responsibility earlier for Chicken Little's death.

Hannah's dress catches fire. (The reader remembers the fire that also was a part of Morrison's childhood.) Eva almost dies trying to save her daughter—again equating her love with her responsibility.

The word *watch* surfaces in the chapter "1923" as it did in the chapter "1922." This time the question is whether Sula *watched* Hannah burn or *saw* her mother burn? Did she stop what she was doing and stare as the men did when the women passed them on Carpenter's Road? Was Sula interested or paralyzed? Why did she not exercise responsibility? Was her inaction an indication of a lack of love?

The theme of good and evil, Heaven and Hell, is again present in *Sula*. Plum has been evil with his drug use, and Hannah says she does not like her own daughter; both receive the punishment of fire or Hell. Eva remembers helping Plum with his constipation and receives coolness as a heavenly reward in the summer heat. These "just dues" are reminiscent of Dante's *Inferno*.

To ensure that the reader continues to turn the pages, Morrison leaves the reader wondering why Sula really did nothing as her mother burned.

Study Questions

1. What was the first strange thing that happened?
2. What was the second strange thing that happened?
3. What are Kentucky Wonders?
4. In what year did Eva's husband leave her?
5. What was the number that Eva and Hannah both knew from the dream book?
6. How did Mr. and Mrs. Suggs put out the fire on Hannah?
7. Who saved Eva's life in the hospital?
8. Whom did Eva see not helping Hannah during the fire?
9. How long did Eva curse Willy?
10. What dream did Hannah have before the fire?

Answers

1. The first strange thing that happened was the wind.
2. The second strange thing that happened was when Hannah took the Kentucky Wonders and a bowl into her mother's room.
3. Kentucky Wonders are a type of green bean or string bean.
4. Eva's husband left her in 1895.
5. The number that Eva and Hannah both knew from the dream book was 522.
6. Mr. and Mrs. Suggs put out the fire on Hannah by throwing a tub of hot water—with tomatoes still in it—on the burning woman.
7. Willy Field was the orderly who saved Eva's life in the hospital.
8. Eva saw Sula not helping Hannah during the fire.
9. Eva cursed Willy for 37 years for saving her.
10. Hannah dreamed of a wedding and a red wedding dress.

Suggested Essay Topics

1. Love is an important theme in *Sula*. Discuss the words about love or lack of love evident at this point between Eva and her daughter Hannah, between Sula and her mother Hannah, and between Eva and Plum.

2. Discuss the reactions of Sula and Eva when they see Hannah on fire. Is there a difference? Do one's actions always reflect one's feelings? Explain.

Chapter Six: 1927

New Character:

Jude Greene: *tenor in Mt. Zion's Men Quartet; 20-year-old bridegroom of Nel Wright; waiter at Hotel Medallion; leaves with Sula*

Summary

Helene Wright was tired but happy in preparing for her only daughter's wedding. Not many people in Medallion had church weddings with receptions. Such weddings were expensive; couples married at the courthouse or "took up" with each other. The Wrights mailed no invitations; everyone just came. Those who could afford a gift brought it; those who could not afford a gift could come without one.

Jude Greene, the bridegroom, had wanted to work on the New Road. His job as waiter at the Hotel Medallion was not what he wanted to do with his life. His rage, his determination to take a man's role, and his need of someone to care for him resulted in his asking Nel to marry him. He particularly liked Nel because she was not trying to get him to notice her. When he presented his problems, Nel cared. She accepted his proposal of marriage.

At the wedding, Morrison tells the reader, everyone realized that the deweys had been 48 inches tall for years and would always remain child-like in thought and action.

At the end of the reception the couple danced together and anticipated their first night as husband and wife. Nel sees Sula over Jude's shoulder.

Analysis

Morrison includes many stylistic devices in "1927." An example of connotation is the following:

> "Even Helene Wright had mellowed with the cane, waving away apologies for drinks spilled on her rug and paying no attention whatever to the chocolate cake lying on the arm of her red-velvet sofa."

Alliteration ("...come crashing down on his foot, and when people asked him how come he limped, he could say...") and a metaphor ("Whatever his fortune, whatever the cut of his garment, there would always be the hem...") are some of the ways that Morrison helps to describe the setting, the feelings, and theme of love in "1927."

In describing the wedding and the reception Morrison uses contrasts: old dancing with young; church women tapping their feet; boys dancing with their sisters. Her writing is effective and presents an imagery to make the chapter real to the reader.

The road-building job symbolizes many important things to Jude. It is a way to remain a part of the world even after death. It is a good-paying job and will allow Jude to use his body to advantage. It is a way to find camaraderie. Even an injury from the hard road could be a badge of pride. Symbolism is important to the chapter and to *Sula.*

Racism is an important theme in "1927." Jude is unable to secure the job because of his color. Jude's color symbolizes something objectionable to the employers. The dark color of other Bottom residents also prevents them from getting jobs from the white employers. Instead of the well-built, black men, the employers hire Greeks, Italians, and skinny, white boys to work on the New Road.

Another theme in the chapter is love. Jude does not marry for love. He marries to have someone to care for him. He marries because he cannot have the job he wants and yet he wants to behave as a man. In the previous chapter Eva equates love with responsibility; in this chapter, however, Jude does not marry with love or responsibility as a motive. He uses marriage to achieve an end: his own care. Racism against Jude, in effect, damages the life of others whom he touches.

Nel's wedding is symbolic to her mother. The narrator states that Helene sees the wedding as "...the culmination of all she had been, thought or done in this world..." Morrison uses foreshadowing to indicate that Helene believes that with this wedding, her life's work is over; she writes that "Once this day was over she [Helene] would have a lifetime to rattle around in that house and repair the damage."

Identity is a prevailing theme in the book and in this chapter. Three boys who are different ages, from different ethnic groups, and from different backgrounds are very unlikely to reach the exact same size at the exact same time and to remain that exact same size forever—in body and in mind. The reader wonders if this has really happened or if others have defined the identity of the deweys. It appears that the deweys have allowed themselves to become what others want them to be; Morrison has always been bold about not allowing others to define her own life. The deweys have made no move to become separate from their counterparts; others have not bothered to try to recognize them. Mrs. Reed could not distinguish one dewey from the other even though they looked nothing alike and nothing like anyone before them. The neighborhood refuses to bother to tell them apart. The residents of the Bottom are, in effect, practicing reverse discrimination by saying, "They all look alike." Unlike Nel, after her visit to New Orleans, the deweys never are able to say, "I'm me."

Morrison ends the chapter with foreshadowing and leaves some unanswered questions for the reader.

> "...It would be ten years before they saw each other again, and their meeting would be thick with birds."

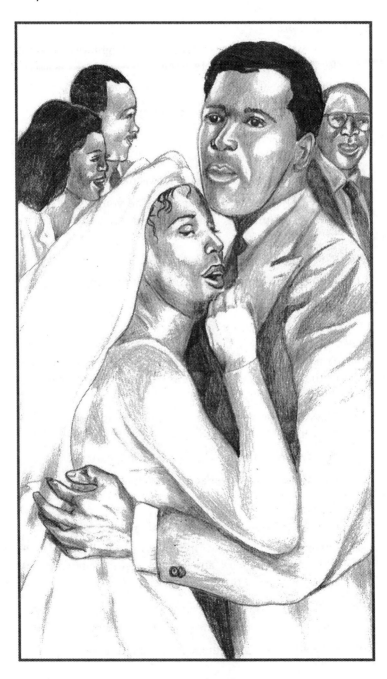

Study Questions

1. What was the social event that Helene Wright was preparing for at the beginning of "1927"?

2. Why did the Wright family not send invitations?

3. In which quartet did Jude Greene sing?

4. Where did Jude work?

5. What job did Jude want?

6. Why did Jude not achieve the job he desired?

7. Why were the old dancing with the young, the church women tapping their feet, and the boys dancing with their sisters?

8. How old was Jude at the wedding?

9. Who left the Bottom at the end of the wedding?

10. When would Sula return to the Bottom?

Answers

1. The social event that Helene Wright was preparing for at the beginning of "1927" was the wedding of her only daughter, Nel.

2. The Wright family did not send invitations because everybody in the Bottom came.

3. Jude Greene sang tenor in the Mt. Zion Quartet.

4. Jude worked as a waiter at the Medallion Hotel.

5. Jude wanted a job as a road builder.

6. Jude did not achieve the job he desired because of his color.

7. The old were dancing with the young, the church women were tapping their feet, and the boys were dancing with their sisters because of the spiked punch.

8. Jude was 20 years old at the wedding.

9. Sula left the Bottom at the end of the wedding.

10. Sula did not return to the Bottom for ten years.

Suggested Essay Topics

1. What were the reasons that Jude asked Nel to marry him? Did any of the reasons have to do with love? Explain.

2. Ajax at the Time and a Half Pool Hall said that with women, "'All they want, man, is they own misery. Ax em to die for you and they yours for life.'" Explain what he meant by this statement. Do you think it is a statement true of all women? Why?

Part Two

Chapter Seven: 1937

New Characters:

John L. and Shirley: *a couple Sula and Nel remember from their youth*

Laura: *the helper who had been living with Eva, Sula, the deweys, and Tar Baby*

Mrs. Rayford: *the next-door neighbor to Nel and Jude*

Summary

Accompanied by a plague of robins, Sula returned to the Bottom ten years after the wedding of Nel and Jude. The people of the Bottom did nothing to rid themselves of the plague. Their attitude was that one must learn to withstand evil.

Eva reprimanded Sula for staying away for ten years and suggested that Sula had only contacted her when she needed something. The argument escalated and Sula stated that Eva put her leg under a train to collect the insurance money; Eva denied the story and reminded Sula to honor her father and mother. Sula said that her mother must not have honored her parents because her days were short; to this, Eva responded, "'Pus mouth! God's going to strike you!'" Sula asked if Eva were referring to the same god that had watched Eva burn her son. The argument became

even more intense. Eva admitted seeing Sula watch Hannah burn. In the heat of the argument Sula threatened to burn Eva.

Eva locked herself in her room, but the lock did not prevent Sula's inevitable destruction of the older woman. Men came with a stretcher, strapped Eva in, and took her to a home near Beechnut.

Nel looked at the return of Sula with joy. She believed that Sula had brought magic to her life. Sula and Nel discussed and laughed about past times. They laughed about how they had scrambled trying to do "it" and not to do "it" at the same time when they were young. They laughed about John L. and Shirley and how the two had tried to do "it."

Sula told of asking Laura to leave their home—even though Laura was working without pay. Sula explained to Nel that she had completed college in Nashville during part of the ten years that she was away from the Bottom. Sula said that she had Eva committed to the home because Sula feared that Eva might burn her, as she had Plum. Sula said that she had witnessed Eva torching Plum. She asked Nel to help her with cashing Eva's checks.

Sula was still in Nel's house when Jude returned from work. Jude told of some insults at work, but before Nel could commiserate, Sula began to explain that whites respected black men in many ways. Jude commented that he could do without respect that resulted in the loss of his privates. Jude's thoughts were that Sula could not stimulate a man's body, but she might stimulate his mind.

In the bedroom, Nel caught Sula and Jude kissing without their clothes and on their hands and knees. Jude left with Sula. Nel was devastated—yet she could not cry. Sula had said that Hell was forever, but Nel found her Hell was change. To cope on a day-to-day basis, Nel found it necessary to avoid the furry, gray ball of string that was in her life.

Analysis

The setting is an integral part of "1937." When Sula returns home to her neighborhood in the Bottom, she meets primarily the stares—not the welcomes—of the neighbors. Sula's reaction to the hills and its residents is that she has managed not to strangle anyone yet. When Nel asks if anyone in the Bottom needs killing, Sula responds that half the town needs killing and the rest of the town is a disease. These reactions to the neighbors foreshadow events to come.

Although the chapter title—like many of the other sections of *Sula*—seems to suggest a chronological treatment of the material, the reader finds that the arrangement is not sequential. The conversations of Sula and Nel use flashbacks as they recall an earlier time in the same place. Morrison uses foreshadowing which hints of future events through the interpretation of the birthmark over Sula's eye.

The birthmark begins to change its form in the eye of the beholder. There is symbolism in this mark and its interpretation by others. In the beginning of the chapter, the birthmark looks like a darker rose to Nel; the mark gets darker, in Nel's eyes, as Sula and she age. Nel's children see the mark as black and scary; they believe that the mark actually leaps. Their interpretation of this mark is foreshadowing of events which will change their lives and their family. Later in the chapter the mark, to Jude, takes on the shape of a copperhead—a silent symbol of danger—when Sula is quiet; when Sula begins to talk, Jude observes the mark again and notes that it resembles a rattler—a noisy symbol of danger. The change in shape of the mark seems to correspond with Sula's behavior and with the perception that others have of her. This symbol is one that appears throughout the book and one that reflects many of the events to come.

Jude's tie hanging over the closet door is symbolic. The tie serves as proof to Nel that Jude was once there; it is the only tangible item that Jude left. The tip of the tie pointing steadily downward is also symbolic of Jude's impotence—his inability to succeed in work, in life, in marriage.

Morrison does not use chronological order in presenting this chapter. Nel and Sula discuss the past. With the discussion, the reader glimpses an earlier time. The writer also gives a hint of what is to come (foreshadowing) in Nel's life by her thoughts about her thighs:

> "...What good are they, Jesus? They will never give me the peace I need to get from sunup to sundown, what good are they, are you trying to tell me that I am going to have to go all

the way through these days all the way, O my god, to that box with four handles with never nobody settling down between my legs... .O my sweet Jesus what kind of cross is that?"

Morrison uses many stylistic devices in her writing. Alliteration (the repetition of sounds) is evident when Morrison describes the robins as "flying and dying." The dialect of the people makes for realistic reading; for instance, a little boy says, "Carry yo' bag, ma'am?" Morrison uses symbolism to describe Nel's feelings upon Sula's return. Nel says that having Sula home was like getting an eye back; the implication is that Sula helped Nel to see the world in proper perspective.

The acceptance of good and evil by those in the Bottom continues in "1937." The residents do not try to eliminate the plague of robins, the symbols of evil. The commonly accepted belief of those in the Bottom is that the purpose of evil is to help one to survive. Those in the hills of Medallion accept the plague of robins, just as they have accepted many misfortunes in the past.

The birds of Medallion symbolize death, as well as evil. The "plague of robins" which accompanies Sula into town also is a foreshadowing of the plague of deaths that will come later in the book. The four robins on the walk into Eva's home symbolize the deaths of the residents of the house: Plum, Sula, Hannah, and Eva.

Sula affects many of the residents upon her return. The following statement foreshadows Sula's influence: "...a relatively trivial phenomenon could become sovereign and bend their minds to its will." They seemingly accept Sula and her return as they do other things in their life.

Morrison employs imagery in her depiction of the tryst between Sula and Jude:

> "...But they had been down on all fours naked, not touching their lips right down there on the floor where the tie is pointing to, on all fours like (uh huh, go on, say it) like dogs. Nibbling at each other, not even touching, not even looking at each other, just their lips, and when I opened the door they didn't even look for a minute... ."

To reveal the characters more fully to the reader, Morrison uses a variety of techniques. She goes into the minds of certain characters and reveals to the reader what they are thinking. After Jude comes in from work and talks with Sula and Nel in the kitchen, Morrison tells the reader that Jude is thinking that Sula could stir a man's mind, but not his body. The reader also knows the depths of Nel's despair when Morrison reveals Nel's thoughts about Jude's departure. The actions of the characters (for example, Jude's and Sula's encounter on the floor), Jude's departure, Nel's inability to speak, and Jude's quick speech (for instance, "I'll be back to get my things."), reveal the characters in depth to the reader. Through contrasts, Morrison explores the differences in the beliefs of Sula and Nel: Sula says that the real Hell is forever and Nel says that Hell is change. The humor that Nel and Sula share on Sula's return tells the reader about the two characters and also provides a flashback of an earlier time.

The reader finds that Sula remains an unpredictable character. Nel seems to have met the Hell that she has dreaded: change. Sula seems to have avoided, for the time being, the Hell that she has dreaded: sameness. The reader received a hint that Sula would find comfort in many men; just as her mother took many different men into the pantry many years before with Sula looking on, Sula finds that many different men are important to her and to her avoidance of sameness.

It is significant that this chapter is the only chapter in the book which contains humor. The recollections of Sula and Nel, their comments on the memories, and their laughter bring some fun into a work which one can only construe as a tragedy.

The reader watches while the tight web of love about Nel's heart unravels along with her life when Jude leaves. To enable the reader to experience Nel's pain, Morrison shifts the narrative voice to first-person to reflect Nel's inner thoughts.

Morrison tempts the reader to read further with an open-ended chapter. There are many unanswered questions. The reader does not know if Jude will return, what will happen to Sula, and if Nel will survive her loss.

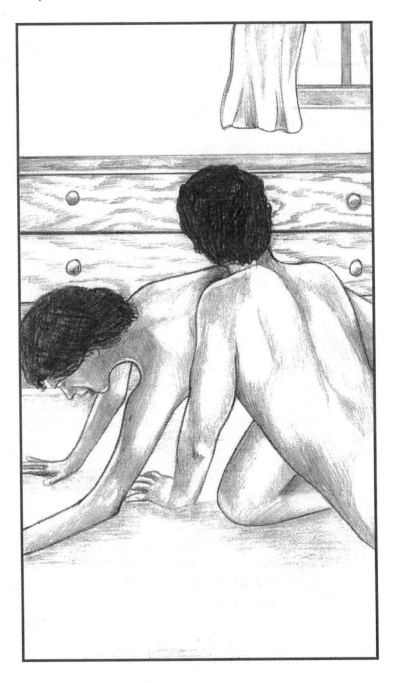

Study Questions

1. How long did it take for Sula to return to the Bottom after Nel's wedding?

2. What plague accompanied Sula?

3. Why did the people of the Bottom do nothing to rid themselves of the plague?

4. How did Sula get Eva out of the house?

5. What did Sula tell Nel that she had witnessed with Eva?

6. How did Nel feel about the return of Sula?

7. Why was Nel surprised that Sula had asked Laura to leave?

8. Where had Sula attended college?

9. Why did Sula tell Nel she had moved Eva into the home?

10. With whom did Jude leave?

Answers

1. It took Sula ten years to return to the Bottom after Nel's wedding.

2. A plague of robins accompanied Sula into the Bottom.

3. The people of the Bottom did nothing to rid themselves of the plague because they believed that they had to learn to live with evil.

4. Sula got Eva out of the house by signing the papers and having the men come with their stretcher to transport Eva to Beechnut.

5. Sula told Nel that she had witnessed Eva burning Plum.

6. Nel greeted the return of Sula with joy and gladness.

7. Nel was surprised that Sula had asked Laura to leave because Laura was receiving no pay for her work.

8. Sula had attended college in Nashville.

9. Sula told Nel she had moved Eva into the home because she was afraid that Eva would burn her as Eva had burned Plum.

10. Jude left with Sula.

Suggested Essay Topics

1. Discuss the symbolism in the mark above Sula's eye.

2. Nel and Sula had different views as to what Hell is. Give their two definitions. Explain what you think each woman meant. Try to specify examples.

Chapter Eight: 1939

New Characters:

Teapot: *five-year-old son of Betty*

Betty: *often called Teapot's Mama because mothering was her major failure in life; reforms and becomes a good mother for a while; relapses*

Mr. Finley: *was sucking on a chicken bone when he saw Sula and choked*

Dessie: *Big Daughter Elk; saw Shadrack tip his imaginary hat to Sula and developed a sty on her eye afterward*

Ivy and Cora: *Dessie's friends*

Ajax's mother: *the only thing Ajax had ever loved besides airplanes*

Summary

The people of the Bottom talked about Sula. They were angry with her for taking Eva to Sunnydale and for leaving with Jude. Sula soon ditched Jude and he went to Detroit. Sula returned to the Bottom. Residents of the Bottom forgot their own easy ways and called Sula a bitch.

The people of the Bottom had the same venom toward integration as the white people. The men in the Bottom gave Sula the final label—the label which would remain with her for life; the conclusive fingerprint, the black men of the Bottom said, was that Sula would sleep with white men. There was nothing filthier in the eyes of the blacks than this integration. The people of the Bottom insisted that any union between a white man and a black woman was rape. For a black woman to agree to such a union was unthinkable.

The rumor may not have been true, but it could have been. After this label, the women pursed their lips, the children looked away with shame, and the young men fantasized torture for Sula whenever she came in sight.

The people did not try to harm her. They merely looked at evil and let it exist. They did sprinkle salt on their steps and lay broomsticks across their doors at night. They watched her carefully and things began to happen.

First, Teapot, the five-year-old of a negligent mother named Betty, came to ask for bottles from Sula. He slipped and fell. Betty was coming home drunk and saw Teapot on the ground. She told everyone that Sula pushed Teapot. Betty took Teapot to the county hospital. For two dollars she found out that Teapot had a fracture resulting in part from his soft bones, a result of inadequate nutrition. Betty became a devoted mother. She became clean and sober. She began to prepare breakfast instead of sending Teapot to get a breakfast of candy and pop.

Second, Mr. Finley was on his porch sucking on a chicken bone when Sula passed by. He looked at her, choked, and died.

Sula continued to antagonize the people of the Bottom. She came to church suppers with no underwear and did not praise the food the people prepared. Sula used the husbands. She took the men once and then cast them aside; her rejection disturbed the wives. The wives had to comfort their husbands and to justify their own choice of their husbands to themselves and others.

Sula did not look her age. She was near 30 and yet she had lost no teeth. She had no ring of fat at her waist and no bruises on her body. The rumor was that she had had no childhood disease. She had no scar on her body except for a deformed finger and a birthmark. The men reported that no gnats or mosquitoes came near Sula in the summer. When the people of the Bottom looked at the mark over Sula's eye, they decided the mark looked like Hannah's ashes.

The people of the Bottom had other rumors to report about Sula. Patsy reported that even when Sula drank beer she did not burp. Dessie saw Shadrack tip his imaginary hat to Sula and afterward Dessie developed a sty for the first time in her life. Dessie identified Sula as the source of her misfortune.

The people of the Bottom, as a result of Sula, began to protect and love each other again. They repaired their homes against the devil and loved each other against the evil one. They did not try to kill or destroy the devil, however. They considered such actions both unnatural and undignified things to do. They believed that they had to be provoked to kill on impulse; otherwise evil was, to the people of the Bottom, something they had to recognize, deal with, survive, outwit, and triumph over in their time.

The evidence against Sula was contrived evidence. The conclusions that the people of the Bottom drew about Sula were not, however, wrong. Sula was different. She felt no obligation to please anyone unless their pleasure pleased her. She was as willing to feel pain as to give pain. She had lived an experimental life because she heard the remark from her mother. She had felt responsibility once when Chicken Little drowned, but Nel had exorcised this responsibility from her. Sula could not, therefore, count on others or herself. Sula had Eva's arrogance and Hannah's self-centeredness.

Sula had not meant to hurt Nel. The two had always shared the affection of others. In the past they had discussed other women and men. They had figured wives did not want their husbands to be unfaithful simply because the wives feared they might lose their job as wives.

Sula was not materialistic, but Nel seemed to want everything. She was like others who climbed the ladder.

As a result of Sula's travels to Nashville, Detroit, New Orleans, New York, Philadelphia, Macon, and San Diego, she had found that all people were the same. They shared only worry with her; they taught her only love tricks; they gave her only money. She wanted a friend. A lover could not fulfill her needs. She was like an artist with no art form; she was dangerous.

Sula lied only once: to Nel about the reason for putting Eva out. To Sula, social conversation was impossible because she could not lie.

Sula was pariah, Morrison says. She liked sex as a comedy and liked to think sex was wicked, not ugly. She rejected those who thought sex was healthy and beautiful. Sula could participate in the act, however, even when she was not thinking the act was wicked. She felt strength and power when she was under someone. Sula went to bed with men to find the misery and deep sorrow she desired. She found loneliness and the death of time. The loneliness she experienced assumed an absence of people; in her solitude she never admitted there could be people. The overt action she employed was to weep. Her partner assumed that he had brought her to tears; she, however, waited for him to turn away so she could meet herself.

When Sula was 29, she heard a step and saw the beautiful black face of Ajax. He had watched her years ago when she was 12, and he was 21. He had at last come to her door with two quarts of milk. Sula stated that she did not drink milk, but Ajax reminded her that the bottle itself was beautiful. Ajax presented her with the bottle after drinking some of the contents, discarding the rest, and rinsing the bottle. Sula went into the pantry with him.

From that time, Ajax came regularly to visit Sula. He brought gifts: berries, fried fish, ice, cleanser, and other small trophies. Ajax was nice to women. The side he presented to women was quite different from the side others often saw: he yelled filthy remarks, he shot at Mr. Finley for beating his own dog, and he lounged in the pool hall. Ajax's attitude toward women was a habit he had from dealing with his mother—the only interesting woman he had ever really met.

Ajax's mother was an evil conjure woman. Her seven children brought her what she needed for her hexes and potions. Ajax's mother made a modest living through her work. She could have been a beautiful woman if she had not lost her teeth and if she had straightened her back. She gave her sons freedom and knowledge. Ajax loved only two things: his mother and airplanes.

Sula experienced pleasure from Ajax. They could carry on good conversations together. He expected brilliance from Sula, and she complied.

Sula maintained her interest in Ajax for several reasons. He was comfortable in her presence. He willingly told her about plants and "fixes." He was unwilling to coddle her. He was generous and only occasionally resorted to vengeance.

Sula did not perhaps feel love for Ajax, but she did feel desire for him. This was a new feeling for her. She recognized her feeling toward Ajax when she wondered if he would stop by her home, when she wondered how she looked, and when she tied a ribbon in her hair, cleaned the house, and set the table for two.

When Ajax came to her, he told her that Tar Baby had stumbled drunk into traffic. The mayor's niece had swerved to miss him and had hit another car. The police arrested Tar Baby. Ajax and two other men went to see Tar Baby. They found him beaten, lying in a corner, and wearing only soiled underclothes. When the three men asked why Tar Baby was in such a state, angry words flew. The result was that the three black men had a civil court date on Thursday next.

Sula invited Ajax to her bathroom, and he began to feel regret. He left her so completely alone that she found it difficult to believe that he was ever there. The only proof came from his driver's license, tucked away in a drawer. She remembered his many layers as she read the statistics on the license and learned his real name, Albert Jacks, for the first time

Analysis

The theme of identity runs throughout the chapter—and throughout *Sula*. Betty has no identity of her own at the beginning of the chapter. The reader learns that even though her name is Betty, she is known primarily as Teapot's mother. Through her brief encounter with Sula, Betty begins to assume her own identity; she tells the community about Sula and the community listens to her. She begins to assume her responsibilities as a mother to Teapot. Betty is, therefore, a dynamic, or changing, character in this chapter.

Morrison uses several stylistic devices to enhance her writing in "1939." For example, Morrison uses a simile when she says that Sula is "like any artist with no art form." Morrison makes use of comparisons and contrasts when she writes that "the narrower a woman's life, the wider her hips." The chapter also contrasts Sula with the other residents of the Bottom. Morrison uses a metaphor when she writes, "She [Sula] was pariah..." Morrison uses personification when she describes the absence of Ajax as "giving" color and "stinging everything." Diction is also evident when Sula remembers the words that Ajax used: "pig meat," "brown sugar," "jailbait," and "Do, Lord, remember me."

Morrison uses symbolism with the bottles of milk. Sula remarks that she does not drink milk—the contents of the bottles. She is actually rejecting a deep, rich, meaningful, complete relationship with another person. Ajax reminds her that the physical container is beautiful also. He is saying that even if one does not pursue a complete relationship, the physical relationship can be a beautiful thing by itself. Ajax drinks some of the milk to show the safety of it. He discards some of it to show that a complete relationship is not a requirement with him. He presents her with the container—the outside trappings of a relationship. Sula accepts the physical portion of the relationship and draws him into the pantry as she saw her mother draw men into the same pantry in the past.

In the earlier chapter, "1921," Sula learns that sex is pleasant, frequent, and otherwise unremarkable. This foreshadowing is complete in Sula's experiences with many men. Sula begins in this chapter to find a change in her life: she begins to feel a possessiveness toward Ajax. She had previously scorned Nel's possessiveness of Jude.

The reader meets Ajax's mother through the narrator's voice. The narrator tells the reader that Ajax's mother is an "evil conjure" woman. This lack of objectivity on the part of the narrator affects the reader's opinion toward the character. Perhaps Morrison's writing about Ajax's mother and her work reflects Morrison's own knowledge of superstition.

The narrator is able to go into the mind of Sula and Ajax. Readers know Ajax's and Sula's thoughts. Limited omniscience helps develop fully certain characters and makes other characters remain flat to the reader.

The previous chapter suggested that Sula liked to have a man above her and described the sad feelings she had during their physical relationship. In this chapter, however, the reader finds that Sula lies above Ajax on the bed and finds joy—not sadness—in their relationship. There is symbolism in the fact that with other men, Sula assumes a position beneath, but with Ajax she assumes a superior position. In the inferior position she is moved to tears; in the superior position, she finds happiness. It is when Ajax decides to leave that he assumes the superior position and she the inferior one.

The reader knows Sula will be sad again when the act is complete. The reader senses that Ajax no longer respects Sula as an individual and an equal. He will not be a possession. Ajax is beginning to treat Sula in a different way. She is an object, perhaps as disposable as the milk bottles Ajax brought to her on his first visit.

Morrison uses limited omniscience. She allows the reader to know the thoughts of some of her characters. Sula, for instance, describes the man, Ajax, and his many valuable layers: gold leaf, alabaster, loam. Her thoughts of layers seem to indicate that as she digs deeper and finds out more about Ajax, he becomes even more valuable to her. There is more to him than just what meets the eye.

Morrison has her characters speak indirectly at times. They do not always say exactly what they mean (denotation) but instead use connotation when they speak. For instance, when Ajax leaves, Sula finds his license and discovers his real name. She remarks:

> "...I didn't even know his name. And if I didn't know his name, then there is nothing I did know and I have known nothing ever at all since the one thing I wanted was to know his name so how could he help but leave me since he was making love to a woman who didn't even know his name."

The reader begins to see another reflection of the background of Morrison in this chapter. When the neighborhood begins to associate Sula with evil, they respond by warding off her evil by placing broomsticks in their doorways and sprinkling salt on the steps into their homes. This superstition relates to the dream books and other superstitious beliefs of Morrison's childhood. The community, in effect, unites against evil. They are taking action—which is new for them. They temporarily change in reaction to Sula.

As with many of her earlier chapters, Morrison continues to use an open ending. One must read the entire novel to find the answers to the many questions raised in the sections. *Sula*, then, is non-episodic. Rather, it is a suspenseful novel which requires one to continue to read.

Study Questions

1. What does it mean when Ajax had the conviction that Sula would very soon "like all of her sisters before her, put to him the death-knell question 'Where have you been?'"

2. Why was Betty angry with Sula?

3. What was Betty's child's name?

4. What had Dessie seen that upset her?

5. What was Ajax's real name?

6. At his arrest, what were the charges against Tar Baby?

7. Why did Ajax leave Sula?

8. What did Mr. Finley do that angered Ajax?

9. What was the first gift that Ajax brought Sula?

10. What item did Sula find which helped her to know that Ajax was not a dream?

Answers

1. Ajax had the conviction that Sula would very soon "like all of her sisters before her, put to him the death-knell question 'Where have you been?'" This meant that Sula would soon try to control or possess Ajax.

2. Betty was angry with Sula because she believed Sula pushed her son.

3. Betty's child's name was Teapot.

4. Dessie was upset because she saw Shadrack tip his imaginary hat to Sula.

5. Ajax's real name was Albert Jacks.

6. The charges against Tar Baby at his arrest were those of drunkenness.

7. Ajax left Sula because he thought she would become bossy and try to control him.

8. Mr. Finley angered Ajax by beating his own dog.

9. The first gift that Ajax brought Sula was two bottles of milk.

10. The item that Sula found that helped her to know that Ajax was not a dream was Ajax's driver's license.

Suggested Essay Topics

1. Explain the following statements that Sula makes:

    "...I didn't even know his name. And if I didn't know his name, then there is nothing I did know and I have known nothing ever at all since the one thing I wanted was to know his name so how could he help but leave me since he was making love to a woman who didn't even know his name."

2. What did Sula mean when she said that she had sung all the songs that there are and that there are no new songs?

Chapter Nine: 1940

New Character:

Nathan: *the school-age child who checks on Sula and who runs errands for her periodically; discovers her lifeless body.*

Summary

After three years, Nel was at last going to meet with Sula face-to-face. She would say that she had heard Sula was sick and would ask if there was anything she could do for her. She practiced her words and would try to insert no inflection into the statements. Yet there would be resentment and shame in her heart when she spoke. She thought of the black rose that Jude had kissed and of her own almost selfish love of her children. For these children Nel had cleaned houses and worked as a chambermaid in the same hotel where Jude had once worked.

At 7 Carpenter's Road, Nel saw Sula's rose, her thin arms, and the bedroom window through which Eva had jumped. Sula asked Nel to pick up a prescription for her as if no time had passed since they last spoke.

The medicine that Sula asked Nel to have filled was a powerful pain-relieving drug. Sula had instructions not to use the medication until the pain was unbearable. Sula gave Nel no money to pay for the medicine; in fact, Nel noticed that the purse holding the prescription was empty except for a watch.

In her errand, Nel walked the street that she and Sula walked years before. She passed the place where she first heard words from Ajax. Sula, meanwhile, wondered why Nel had come.

Upon Nel's return they first discussed Sula's staying alone and working. Sula remarked that work was good for Nel but that she herself would not work. Nel remarked that Sula never had to work.

Nel said she could not act like a man. Sula retorted that she was "a woman and colored" and asked if that was not the same as being a man. Nel told Sula that Sula would not think that being a woman and colored was the same as being a man if she had children. Sula remarked that if she had children she really would be like a man; every man she had ever known had left his children.

Nel chastised Sula for knowing everything and for not knowing what Nel had gone through. In response, Sula said that she knew what every colored woman was doing: dying, the same as she was. Sula said, however, that there was a difference: She was like a redwood while other women were like stumps. She likened herself to a redwood because of what was going on in her mind and because of the life that she had lived. Sula concluded by saying that she had herself.

Nel flippantly remarked that it must be lonely for Sula with just herself. Sula said that it was, but that she was responsible for her loneliness; Nel, on the other hand, blamed someone else for her loneliness. Sula called Nel's feelings a secondhand kind of loneliness. Even though Nel did not know the physical condition of Sula, she decided to go ahead and tell "the truth." Nel said she was at last able to understand why Sula had been unable to keep a man, but she always knew how she could take a man.

When Sula asked what was she supposed to do (keep a man), Nel responded that men were worth keeping. Sula retorted that men were not worth more than she herself was. Nel said that Sula thought she owned the world and the rest of the people just rented. Nel went on to say that she had not come for "this kind of talk," but had come to see about Sula; because Sula had opened things up, however, Nel asked why she had done it.

Sula responded that Jude had merely filled a space. Nel, horrified, asked if Sula had taken Jude without even loving him and why Sula had done that to her. Sula, matter-of-factly, said loving someone was like being mean to someone: risky. Sula said she had not taken Jude away; she had merely had intercourse with him. Sula said that if Nel had really loved her as a true friend, Nel would have forgiven her.

Nel reminded Sula that she was in a bed without a friend or any money and she was expecting others to love her. Sula predicted that in time others would love her. Sula said that at some time in the future there would be love left over for her, and she knew what it would feel like.

When Nel was preparing to leave, she warned Sula that she may not return. Sula left her with a parting question: how did Nel know that she was the good one?

Nel walked away and thought of the deweys who were living anywhere, of Tar Baby who was still drinking, of Eva in Sunnydale, and of Sula with no money, a boarded-up window, and an empty pocketbook.

Sula knew that Nel would walk on in the old coat, with her back straight, and never remember the days of "two throats and one eye." She recalled seeing Hannah burn but remembered that she was thrilled to see her mother dance. Sula experienced wires, throbs, and explosions of pain before she died, alone as she had always wanted to be.

In Sula's near-death condition she strives to reach the rain, or the water, at the end of the tunnel. She imagines the water will envelop her, carry her, and wash her always. She tries to recall the one who had said the word "always" to her in an earlier time and place.

Sula's last thoughts were that death had not hurt, and she could not wait to tell that to Nel.

Analysis

The setting for the chapter has not changed from any of the chapters before it. The Bottom remains an integral part of "1940." The Peace home is the place where Sula and Nel meet for the last time.

Morrison allows the reader to enter the minds of both Sula and Nel in this chapter. Both think of earlier, happier times, as well as the time that Nel initially sees as one of betrayal.

Sula regrets that Nel will not think back on the times when they "were two throats and one eye." This metaphoric expression is symbolic of the times when they had talked with one another and had seen things alike, or with one eye.

Diction between the two women and former friends is an important part of the chapter. In fact, the chapter "1940" contains more conversation than any other section of the book to this point. The realistic diction of Nel and Sula includes such phrases as, "Hey, girl" and "How come you did it, Sula?" The two throats (Sula and Nel) again express their true feelings, but they do not view things in the same way (with one eye) as they once did.

Morrison uses other expressions to make the feelings and settings real to the reader. For instance, she uses a metaphor ("wires of liquid pain") to describe the pain that Sula feels. Morrison uses personification when she tells the reader that Sula's pain "was joined by fatigue." Sula uses an effective simile when she likens herself to a redwood and the other women to stumps.

Several important themes emerge in "1940"; one of these is love. Nel blames Sula for taking Jude away from her and for making her focus all her love on her children. She refers to this love as a "cumbersome bear-love" which "would suck their breath away in its crying need for honey." This description helps the reader to imagine the loss that Nel has endured and the intensity of the emotion and affection that Nel now focuses on her offspring. Nel's identity is not as complete as it was after New Orleans; Nel defines herself through others.

Nel and Sula discuss their concepts of love in their last conversation. Nel is curious as to how Sula could have left with her husband if Sula really loved her. Sula also believes that Nel should have forgiven if she truly loved her friend and husband. Sula said that love is "risky." Nel asks Sula how she can expect others to love her with her actions. Sula replies that others will love her after all. After she is gone, they will love her. Sula even says she knows how this love will feel.

The theme of change is a second theme in this chapter. This theme has occurred frequently in other chapters throughout the book. Morrison, through the narrator, observes that nothing is ever different. Sula mourns that the sun is the same one she has always observed, her smell is the same, and her hair follicles are unchanged; in an earlier conversation with Nel, Sula has remarked that Hell would be sameness. It appears that Sula is now condemned to sameness from her sickbed. Nel, however, is experiencing much change—Nel's idea of Hell.

Loneliness is a third important theme. Sula says that Nel's "lonely" is somebody else's "lonely"; in other words, Nel has not taken charge of her life. She has allowed someone else (her husband, her children, Sula) to control her feelings. Sula, on the other hand, has had control of her life. She is alone, but she is alone chiefly by her own doing—not by anyone else's actions. This explanation reminds the reader of Sula's not allowing anyone else to determine her feelings toward herself. Morrison professes also to control how she feels about herself.

The fourth important theme in this chapter, in *Sula*, and in many works of Morrison is that of innocence. When the two former friends are speaking of why Sula used Jude, Sula seems neither to show regret nor to acknowledge wrong-doing. Nel thinks that talking to Sula about right and wrong is like talking to the deweys; this analogy indicates that both Sula and the deweys (who never grew up and remained children in mind, body, and spirit) may be innocent. Nel still blames Sula; she does not tell Sula that it is not Sula's fault as she did by the river when Sula accidentally drowned Chicken Little. Sula asks Nel at the end of their visit how Nel can know who is good. Sula says that maybe it is she herself—not Nel—who has been good; perhaps Sula is innocent and not accountable.

Even though Sula is facing death, she still seems satisfied that she has lived her own life and that perhaps her way has been good.

The reader finds out even more about Sula—and Nel—through their conversations with each other, through their reactions to and actions with each other, and through their thoughts. Morrison continues to reveal her characters in a variety of ways and, in doing so, makes them real. For instance, Nel's posture (back straight), Nel's harsh words to Sula, Nel's thoughts as she goes for the medication, and Sula's reactions and words to Nel reveal more about Nel—and Sula.

The symbolism of the rose is again prominent in Morrison's writing. This time the rose is black. In prior chapters the rose has been a stemmed rose, a copperhead, a rattlesnake, and Hannah's ashes. The black rose symbolizes a rose that is dying. It is no longer vibrant like a stemmed rose or alive like a copperhead or rattle-snake. The black rose is at the end of its journey; the dark, black color is a symbol of death.

There is symbolism in Nel's name. The reader begins to wonder if Nel Wright is truly right. Sin and evil, in this chapter, seem to be actions committed against what one believes is right for one's own self. Sin and evil do not necessarily relate to actions typical of a particular religion. Sula is adamant about acting in the way that is best for her; Nel, on the other hand, has allowed others to control her life.

The reader, however, begins to wonder if Sula has really always chosen her own actions. She patterned her sex life after that of her mother. She felt pain as a child when she overheard her mother's comments about her; perhaps the careless death of Chicken Little was actually a result of her preoccupation with her mother's words. She felt concern about the loss of Ajax—much as Nel had with the loss of Jude earlier in the book.

Blue glass is a part of the house on 7 Carpenter's Road. Morrison used blue glass earlier in her writing when she described the blue glass of the milk bottles that Ajax brings when he visits Sula for the first time. The glass milk bottles symbolized a superficial relationship. The blue glass in the house on 7 Carpenter's Road also symbolizes the now superficial relationship existing between Sula and Nel. The mention of the blue glass is a foreshadowing of what is to come during Nel and Sula's last visit.

In "1940," Morrison makes good use of flashback and foreshadowing. On her way to get the prescription for Sula, Nel remembers where Sula and she first heard Ajax's estimation of them. Both Nel and Sula remember the past and talk about it in their last encounter. The use of flashback brings nostalgia to both of them for what once was. Sula remembers the time that they dug the graves with the sticks—just before the death of Chicken Little. This flashback foreshadows another grave—that belonging to Sula.

Further foreshadowing is evident when Sula can hardly wait to tell Nel that death is painless; this is a hint—a foreshadowing—that there will be a later reunion between the two.

Morrison again employs foreshadowing when she allows the reader to enter the mind of Sula in her near-death condition. Just as Eva remarks that Plum was trying to enter her womb again, Sula, too, seems to be trying to move through a tunnel to find the water, amniotic fluid, or refuge to protect and envelop her always. Morrison implies that safety and peace could be within the mother's body, but that another refuge "at the end of the tunnel" might also exist.

Morrison's writing style in "1940" helps the reader experience Sula's death. Morrison reveals Sula's feelings, her smells, and her thoughts in this graphic picture. Metaphors (placed in bold) and personification (placed in italics) abound in her description. For example:

> "...she woke gagging and overwhelmed with the smell of smoke.
>
> *Pain* took hold. Once the **wires of liquid pain** were in place, they jelled and began to throb. She tried concentrating on the throbs, identifying them as **waves, hammer strokes, razor edges or small explosions**...it was joined by *fatigue*..."

The reader has a sense of satisfaction at the end of the chapter to find that the experience of dying has actually not hurt, that Sula dies smiling, and that she plans to tell Nel in the future about her encounter with death. The reader must continue reading to find out who finds Sula's body, what Nel's reaction will be, and what will become of Medallion and the people there.

Study Questions

1. How long had it been since Nel had last seen Sula when the chapter "1940" begins?
2. Where did Nel find the money to care for her family?
3. At what address did Sula live?
4. What did Sula ask Nel to buy for her?
5. What two things did Nel find in Sula's purse?
6. How did Nel feel about work?
7. How did Sula feel about work?
8. How did Sula say being mean to someone and loving someone were alike?
9. How did Sula say people would eventually feel about her?
10. What news did Sula want to share with Nel at the end of "1940"?

Answers

1. When the chapter "1940" begins, it had been three years since Nel had talked with Sula.
2. Nel found the money to care for her family by cleaning for others.
3. Sula lived at 7 Carpenter's Road.
4. Sula asked Nel to buy a prescription for her.
5. Nel found a watch and a prescription in Sula's purse.
6. Nel felt work did not hurt one.
7. Sula said she never would work.
8. Sula said being mean to someone and loving someone were alike because both were risky.
9. Sula said people would eventually love her.

10. Sula wanted to share with Nel the news that death did not hurt.

Suggested Essay Topics

1. Nel and Sula discuss work. They have different opinions on work. First, explain their views of work. Then, compare and contrast these views. Is one of these women more correct than the other? Why?

2. What is loneliness? Compare and contrast Nel's loneliness and Sula's loneliness. Is one type of loneliness to be preferred? Which one? Why?

Chapter Ten: 1941

New Characters:

Mr. Hodges: *man who hires Shadrack to rake leaves; Shadrack becomes aware of Sula's death when he sees her on a table at Hodges' home*

L.P., Paul Freeman and his brother Jake, Mrs. Scott's twins: *examples of the beautiful boys of 1921*

Summary

The "best news" that the Bottom had had since the tunnel work was the death of Sula. Some came to the funeral to see a witch buried; others came to observe the burial of Sula. Some came to see that nothing inappropriate happened at the funeral; these people wanted to make sure that a gentleness of spirit abided at the last rites. Because Sula was dead or after Sula was dead, most believed a brighter future lay ahead. The two signs of this new day were the announcement of the tunnel to connect with the River Road and the construction of a new home for the aged.

Both signs brought hope to the Bottom. The blacks felt that they may have a chance for employment to help construct the tunnel. It was true the River Road was the result of only white labor, but the government seemed to view favorably the hiring of black workers.

The construction—actually renovation—of the old people's home was good news to the Bottom because black people could reside there. Many viewed the transfer of Eva from a dark, dismal place to the shiny, new facility as the working of God.

Cold weather came to Medallion and the Bottom. The residents of the hills suffered in their poorly insulated homes and shabby clothes. Work was at a standstill, and they could purchase few things. Thanksgiving brought tough poultry, stringy potatoes, and disease for the young and old.

Worse still, the violence and death that Shadrack feared seemed upon them. The violence began when Betty beat Teapot for the worst insult a child can give its mother: refusing the food she offers. In this case, Teapot refused the oleomargarine his mother had failed to mix with the yellow powder before spreading his bread and adding the sugar. Mothers who had once had to defend their roles from Sula's scorn and their children from Sula's rumored harm now had no cause to protect their offspring. Daughters who had cared for their mothers because of Sula's poor example now again felt resentment toward their elders. Wives no longer coddled their mates and Negroes from Canada began again to claim superiority over those born in the South.

Hunger, disease, and cold weather increased the bad temper in the Bottom. Even the fact that four black men received interviews for employment at the tunnel site did not relieve this mean-spiritedness. Hope seemed imminent, however. On January 1 the temperature rose to 61 degrees. On January 2 one could see some patches of grass in the pastures. On January 3 Shadrack brought his bell and his rope and recited his annual request.

Shadrack had changed. He drank less frequently, but his stupors were deeper. He had improved. In fact, as he improved, he even began to feel the emotion of loneliness. His habits of cleanliness, learned in the military, deteriorated. A bird flew into his shack and stayed for an hour before it flew out again. Shadrack grieved for the bird.

Shadrack focused on the purple-and-white belt left by a young girl many years before. He remembered the visit from this girl and his word of "always" to her. He meant this word as a reassurance to her about death and a promise of permanency for her even after death.

Shadrack saw Sula on a table in Mr. Hodges' home. He learned his visitor, his guest, his friend had died. For the first time since his return from France, he did not want to celebrate National Suicide Day.

The next morning, however, he began his ritual walk down Carpenter's Road with very little enthusiasm. For the first time his walk met with laughter. Dessie started the laughter. Ivy picked up the derision. Soon all the people standing on the road to watch the march were laughing. Dessie fell in line behind him first; others joined the parade. The parade seemed to give them hope and allowed them to forget their anxiety for a moment.

Helene Wright viewed the parade with her typical scorn. Some who understood the Spirit refused to join the parade. Some of those who joined the parade began to drop out when they approached the white section of town. The majority, however, continued their trek down Main Street, past Woolworth's, and by the old poultry house. The marchers turned right and approached the New River Road.

At the tunnel the marchers became quiet. The promise, they realized, had been dead since 1927. The parade attacked the tunnel they were unable to help construct. They even entered the tunnel in their frenzy. When the cave-in came, many were crushed; others drowned in the rush of water.

Shadrack stood and rang his bell; he had forgotten his song and his rope.

Analysis

The theme running throughout "1941" is the survival of the unfittest. Shadrack is a survivor in the chapter. Although less fit mentally than many other inhabitants of Medallion because of his injuries on the battlefield in France, Shadrack manages to withstand the social, physical, and emotional trauma about him and continue his life. Many of the other residents are not so fortunate. Morrison has hinted of their deaths in previous chapters.

Morrison describes the death of these residents of Medallion during the collapse of the tunnel. Shadrack has led them to the site of the tunnel and the eventual cave-in. The crowd has become a mob and has taken action into their own hands. They attempt to destroy the "leaf-dead promise" of the tunnel. The reader finds that:

> "All the while Shadrack stood there. Having forgotten his song and his rope, he just stood there high up on the bank, ringing, ringing his bell."

Morrison uses foreshadowing when she says that those who attended the funeral of Sula were unaware of the "bleak promise" of the song "Shall We Gather at the River." It is fitting that Sula's funeral song contains a reference to water because in her near-death state Sula has a vision of water. The water that has symbolized death at several points in the book and that has taken the life of Chicken Little now takes the lives of many of the residents of the Bottom when the tunnel collapses.

The reader finally receives an explanation of one of the questions which has gone unanswered throughout the book. Shadrack used the word "Always" with Sula so she would not be afraid of the death which will come and so she would know that there will be permanency for her. The word *always* and the vision that Shadrack had of her skull foreshadow Sula's death.

Mrs. Jackson, who has craved ice throughout the book, meets with an open mouth the ice inside the tunnel. Her open mouth is symbolic of her welcoming death.

Morrison's descriptive language gives the reader a clear picture of the setting. For example, Morrison says that the town turned silver, to describe the rain that fell and froze. Morrison employs alliteration (in this case the letter *s*); "...sprinkled stove ashes, like ancient onyx, onto the new-minted silver." Similes add to the description in the chapter; for example, she describes the sun looking "like a worn doubloon..." and she writes that "Christmas ...haggled everybody's nerves like a dull ax...." Personification helps to complete the image: "Grass stood blade by blade, shocked into separateness..." Morrison makes a reference to a real-life event immortalized in a poem by Robert Browning ("The Pied Piper of Hamelin") when she describes the parade forming behind

Shadrack as being a "pied piper's band." This use of allusion, or connotation, helps to describe effectively the sight on Carpenter's Road.

The mark above Sula's eye takes on a new shape to Shadrack. To him, the birthmark is a tadpole, his favorite fish. (It is significant that the tadpole is called a fish, associated with water; in reality the tadpole becomes a frog, which is at home on the land and in the water.) Again, the reader sees that those about Sula place on her birthmark their own interpretation of the mark—as well as their interpretation of her identity.

Most of the inhabitants of the Bottom have shown themselves to be capable of only two things: judging Sula and responding to her behavior. This pattern culminates in the final Suicide Day parade. Without Sula as a common enemy against which to unite, the inhabitants of the Bottom return to their petty, insulated lives until Shadrack gives them something to band together for. The inhabitants, like sheep, go off to meet their deaths. This "punishment" is reminiscent of Dante's *Inferno*.

Another prominent symbol in the story is the bird. Birds are symbols of death—especially a bird in the house. The swarming of birds to Medallion when Sula returns after her ten-year absence foreshadows, or warns, the reader of an unpleasant happening or great tragedy to come when many will die. The bird in Shadrack's house also symbolizes the death of Sula, who has been of great importance in Shadrack's life. Shadrack has even kept her belt—a symbol of his visit from her, his company of years past, his social life, his friend.

The tunnel is an important symbol to the people of the Bottom. It symbolizes their worth, their permanence, their fitness, their link to others, and—if they gain employment—camaraderie. When the Bottom residents realize they will not get to participate in the construction, they attack the tunnel, the symbol of their unworthiness to others. Their death in attacking the symbol indicates the futility of their actions. It is ironic that all the deaths from the collapse of the tunnel occur on National Suicide Day.

Shadrack sees Sula on a table in Mr. Hodges' home. Now Shadrack, too, knows of Sula's death. The view of the body on the table upsets Shadrack. The knowledge of her death changes things for him.

The reader is finding in "1941" that Shadrack is not remaining an unchanging, static character any longer; he is becoming a dynamic, changing character.

Loneliness is a theme in "1941." This time, however, loneliness is a positive emotion that Shadrack is well enough to experience.

Ironically, the only link between two inhabitants in the Bottom which remains secure throughout the novel is the friendship between Nel and Sula. The theme of friendship prevails through several decades. It is more lasting than erotic love. Its value to the emotional health of the characters is evident.

It is significant that Helene Wright does not follow Shadrack. She is right in her reaction to the situation, as one would expect someone with the name of *Wright* (right) to be.

At the end of "1940," there are some unresolved conflicts. The reader must go to the last chapter, "1965," to determine the outcome of Medallion and what is going to happen to Nel. Again, the chapter is an open-ended—not a closed—one.

Study Questions

1. What was Sula's last name?

2. What was the hymn sung at Sula's funeral?

3. What were the two things under construction?

4. What did Shadrack see in the birthmark above Sula's eye?

5. What did the purple-and-white belt symbolize for Shadrack?

6. How did Shadrack find out that Sula was dead?

7. Who was the first person to die at the tunnel?

8. How did most of the people react to Shadrack on this National Suicide Day?

9. How did the people begin to treat each other after the death of Sula?

10. How does the reader know that Shadrack was improving?

Answers

1. Sula's last name was Peace.

2. The hymn sung at Sula's funeral was "Shall We Gather at the River."

3. The tunnel and the home for the aged were the two things under construction.

4. Shadrack saw a tadpole in the birthmark above Sula's eye.

5. The purple-and-white belt symbolized a guest, a daughter, a woman, and a social life for Shadrack.

6. Shadrack found out that Sula was dead when he saw her on a table at Mr. Hodges' home.

7. The first person to die at the tunnel was Dessie.

8. Most of the people laughed at Shadrack on this National Suicide Day.

9. The people begin to treat each other with no respect after the death of Sula.

10. The reader knows that Shadrack was improving because he felt loneliness.

Suggested Essay Topics

1. Relate Sula and her last name to the actions of the people in the Bottom after she "pushes" Teapot, commits Eva, and leaves with Jude. Discuss the actions of the people of the Bottom after Sula dies and is no longer in the community.

2. Who was the first person to die in the collapse of the tunnel? What had this person done to Sula? Does her death seem like retribution?

Chapter Eleven: 1965

Summary

Things seemed better in 1965. The colored people were beginning to find work in the stores; one was even teaching in the
local school.

Nel remarked that many things were better in the past.
The young men of the day reminded Nel of the deweys. It was
becoming more difficult for Nel to recognize many of the people
in the town.

Medallion seemed to build a home for the elderly every time
it built a road. It appeared the community needed more rooms for
the elderly. The population was not necessarily living longer; the
families were just placing their elderly in the homes sooner.
It seemed easy for the white families to place their older people in
the homes, but generally the black families did not put their
elderly in a home until they "got crazy and unmanageable." A few
of the blacks, however, were like Sula, and put their elderly away
for meanness.

Up until 1965, Nel had lived a narrow life. She had had a
relationship with a sergeant stationed at a camp near Medallion,
but that relationship had petered out. She had formed a liaison
with a bartender at the hotel, but that did not last long. Nel was 55
in 1965, and it was difficult for her to remember what relationships
were all about.

Nel joined a service circle when her children left home.
Members of her Circle Number 5 often took turns visiting the
elderly. It was her turn, and Nel was walking to the old folks' home.
Nel was curious to see Eva again.

After Jude left, Nel predicted her future. With three children
she would find no other love in her life. The three children, however, were now grown and were looking elsewhere than their
mother for happiness.

The Bottom had changed. Land was expensive. Whites were
looking to expand to the hills. Blacks could not afford to purchase
land in the Bottom if they were not already land owners. The new

home builders in the Bottom were white; they wanted a house with a view of the river and elm trees. Because the blacks wanted to move to the valley, they sold the hill land to anyone who expressed interest. There were only a few close relationships remaining in the Bottom.

Nel was one of the few pedestrians left in the Bottom. Her children laughed at her for walking. She, however, adamantly refused to accept a ride unless the weather required it. To reach the home for the elderly, therefore, Nel walked.

It was four o'clock and chilly when she arrived at Sunnydale. She was eager to sit down and rest for a while. She entered a room with a long hall and doors on either side. She imagined that the building looked like a college dormitory. A receptionist gave her a pass and, after knocking, she entered the third door on the right.

Eva appeared small in her chair at the table. Her once beautiful leg had no stocking and was in a slipper. Nel grieved for the proud foot which was stuffed into terry cloth.

Nel greeted Eva, who imagined herself ironing and was dreaming of stairs. Eva did not stop her imaginary ironing even when she asked Nel to sit. Eva predicted Nel would be sick later in the day—perhaps from eating chop suey; Eva assured Nel that she knew what she was talking about. Nel tried to tell Eva that she had eaten no chop suey. Eva reminded Nel that she—Eva—had come a long way to visit Nel. Eva said Nel would not have come this far just to deny eating chop suey.

Nel explained that she was visiting Eva. Nel tried to identify herself to Eva. Eva asked if she were Wiley Wright's daughter, and Nel was relieved that Eva knew her. Eva asked how Nel had drowned Chicken Little years ago. Nel tried to explain that it had been Sula who had drowned the child; Eva said that it made no difference. Eva explained that water was cold and that fire was warm.

Eva questioned Nel further about the death, and Nel tried to explain that she did not kill Chicken. Eva insisted that she had been talking to sweet Plum and that she knew otherwise. Eva reminded Nel that she had "watched." Eva offered to give Nel some oranges— only now Eva called Nel by the name of Sula.

Nel was upset and walked out of the building with Eva calling, "Sula!" Nel recalled the scene by the river when Chicken Little had drowned. Eva focused on the word *watched*. Nel would have said that she *saw*, but not that she *watched*. Eva had said that Sula had watched Hannah burn; the question had surfaced again. This time the question was if Nel had *watched* Chicken Little drown.

Nel began to have questions about herself. Perhaps the maturity and serenity she displayed upon seeing Chicken Little drown was only tranquillity following a joyful stimulation.

Nel ran to the cemetery where Sula and Plum lay. She read the markers and found they were like a chant. They reduced life and death to mere words, wishes, longings.

Nel had believed for years that she had shared with Eva the feeling of being unloved and lonely. During her visit to the home, Nel began to reexamine her attitude toward Eva. Nel had always believed that Eva refused to attend the funeral of Sula because she did not want to see her family, her flesh, and her blood placed in the earth. Eva, she believed, did not want to see what her heart could not hold.

Nel began to change her beliefs. She now believed that Eva did not attend because Eva was an evil person. Nel thought there was no excuse for Eva to speak so cruelly during the visit. Nel decided that Eva had spoken as she had and refused to attend Sula's funeral because of meanness.

Nathan had found Sula dead in her room. When Nathan announced his find, none of the women or men bothered to go. They ignored the news. Sula's body lay all alone.

Nel recalled how the people in the Bottom had always come together in death, but they had not come to Sula. It had been Nel who had made the calls to the hospital, the funeral home, and the police. The white people had taken charge. Nel had gone to the white funeral parlor but had seen only a closed coffin. This type coffin had shocked Nel, and she had left quickly.

The next day Nel visited the cemetery. She noticed that the white people—Mr. and Mrs. Hodges, their son, and the grave diggers—gathered around the grave. After the whites left the cemetery, the blacks entered the cemetery and gathered around the gravesite. It was at this time that the residents of the Bottom sang the song "Shall We Gather at the River." The song was sung as a question.

Nel left the cemetery with a heavy heart. She met Shadrack, who stopped and tried to remember who she was. When he could not recall, Shadrack ran on to haul the trash out at Sunnydale. Shadrack had not been able to catch or sell fish for some time. The river had killed all the fish.

Nel stopped suddenly. She realized that the sorrow she had felt for all the years after Jude left had been sorrow for the loss of Sula— not sorrow for the loss of Jude. Her final words are, "'O Lord, Sula...girl, girl, girlgirlgirl.'"

Analysis

The narrator of "1965" is Nel. She begins the narration with contradictions. Nel states that things are better in 1965. Then, in direct opposition, she begins to recall the youth of 1921 and remarks that the young people and even the prostitutes were better in the earlier time.

Nel compares the youth of 1965 to the deweys. This comparison shows that she attaches no individuality to the young people that she sees. Likewise, the people of the Bottom in the past had not bothered to recognize the individuality of the deweys.

Eva gives an allusion to the past during Nel's visit. She reminds Nel that water is cold and that fire is warm; Eva seems to suggest that death by fire (Plum) is preferable to death in the water (Chicken Little and the residents who had died by water in the tunnel). The comparison of fire with warmth is an understatement, a stylistic device which puts the comparison between fire and warmth mildly.

Morrison uses imagery when she depicts the inability of Shadrack to fish after the "river had killed the fish." The reader gets a mental picture of the act of fishing that Shadrack misses:

> "...No more silver-gray flashes, no more flat, wide, unhurried look. No more slowing down of gills. No more tremor on the line."

Morrison uses flashback effectively when Nel remembers the scene by the river and the death of Chicken Little. The question of the difference between *seeing* and *watching* arises when Eva asks Nel about the happenings at the river. The reader remembers the

question that Eva raised earlier about whether Sula had *watched* her mother burn.

Morrison's reference to the grave markers reading like a chant is an effective analogy. A chant repeats. Life and death repeat. The markers attest to the repetition of chants and life—and death.

Morrison's analogy between chants and grave markers is evidence of her knowledge of music and chants. The reader remembers from Morrison's childhood that her mother sang, her grandfather played the violin, and Morrison herself planned to become a dancer when she was younger.

To Nel, the people are now only words recorded in a cemetery. The words are actually the wishes and longings never fulfilled in life. The people are gone forever.

The theme of aloneness is evident again in "1965." Nel recalls that when Nathan announced that Sula was dead, no one came. Sula was alone in death and after death, as she had been in life. The people had always come when death occurred, but they did not gather around Sula as they had done even for the community prostitute; neither had they come when she returned to Medallion after college.

Nel, too, was alone. Her husband was gone; her children were gone; her best friend was dead; Eva was not the way that Nel had imagined her to be.

The words of Sula came true. After her death, Nel realizes that she loves Sula. The foreshadowing in an earlier chapter comes to pass.

The theme of "1965" is the survival of the unfittest. The reader finds that Shadrack with his psychological war injury, Eva with her missing leg, and Nel with her grief over losing her husband and best friend are the survivors. Strong Jude, assured Hannah, and confident Sula have not survived in the Bottom.

The genre of *Sula* is indisputably a tragedy. The last words of the novel itself are "...circles and circles of sorrow."

Study Questions
1. Of whom did the young men of 1965 remind Nel?
2. Why were more homes for the elderly necessary in Medallion?

3. How many children did Nel have?

4. What was happening to land in the Bottom in 1965?

5. Nel persisted in doing an activity that most people in the Bottom did not do. What was this activity?

6. What did Eva imagine she was doing when Nel visited?

7. Whom did Eva call Nel at the end of the visit?

8. Whom did Nel meet on the way to the cemetery?

9. What was the song sung at the cemetery for Sula?

10. What food did Eva say that Nel had eaten?

Answers

1. Nel thought the young men of 1965 reminded her of the deweys.

2. More homes for the elderly were necessary because many families were placing their old persons in the homes sooner.

3. Nel had three children.

4. The whites were buying the land in the Bottom in 1965.

5. Nel persisted in walking, an activity that most people in the Bottom did not do.

6. Eva imagined she was ironing when Nel visited.

7. Eva called Nel by the name of Sula at the end of the visit.

8. Nel met Shadrack on her way to the cemetery.

9. The song sung at the cemetery for Sula was "Shall We Gather at the River."

10. Eva said that Nel had eaten chop suey.

Suggested Essay Topics

1. Discuss how the collapse of the tunnel had affected Shadrack.

2. The song "Shall We Gather at the River" was sung as a question. What were the questions suggested by the song?

Sample Analytical Paper Topics

The following paper topics should test your understanding of the novel as a whole and allow you to analyze important themes and literary devices. Following each question is a sample outline to get you started.

Topic #1

The birthmark on Sula's face presents a different image to different people. The meaning of the mark seems to change also because of Sula's actions at the time and because of the events surrounding her. Note each description of the birthmark over Sula's eye. Through whose eye is the reader viewing each of these symbols? What are the circumstances, actions, and reasons surrounding Sula at the time which bring about this image on Sula's face?

Outline

I.   Thesis Statement: *At various times, the mark on Sula's face was a long-stemmed rose (according to the narrator when describing Nel and Sula as children), a symbol of Hannah's ashes (according to residents of the Bottom when Sula comes home after ten years), a rose grown darker (according to Nel when Sula comes home after ten years), a copperhead (according to Jude before Sula speaks upon her return after ten years), a rattler (according to Jude after Sula speaks upon her return after ten years), a black rose (according to Nel upon seeing Sula on her*

*deathbed), and a tadpole (according to Shadrack when he re-
members Sula's visit to his home so long ago and when he sees
her on the table after death).*

II. Described as a long-stemmed rose when Nel and Sula
     are children

    A. Mentioned first in "1922"

    B. Described by the narrator in great detail in "1922"

    C. Included in their Technicolor dreams of a presence, a
        someone who shared their delight in their dreams and
        was interested in flow of hair, thickness of flower mattress,
        voile sleeves, detail of birthmark

    D. Presented as one of Sula's physical characteristics

        1. Had large quiet eyes, one featuring birthmark

        2. Had spread of mark from middle of the lid toward
           the eyebrow

        3. Had shape of rose

        4. Gave Sula a broken excitement

        5. Grew darker as years passed

        6. Contained same shade as gold-flecked eyes

        7. Maintained eyes as steady and clean as rain

III. Described in year 1937

    A. Seen by Nel

        1. Appeared darker than Nel remembered

        2. Gave a suggestion of startled pleasure when she
           looked at Nel

    B. Observed by Nel's children when they studied Sula

        1. Were puzzled by person who made their mother make
           strange laughing sounds

        2. Were fearful of this one who made dark sleepy chuck-
           ling sounds

        3. Saw scary black thing over eye

    4. Saw Sula as threat to them in some way that they did not understand

    5. Saw black mark "leap"

C. Noted also by Jude when he studied Sula

    1. Saw Sula quiet

      a. Looked like woman roaming

      b. Seemed not exactly plain, but not exactly fine

      c. Saw mark as copperhead

    2. Saw Sula differently after she talked and made noise (rattled danger signal)

      a. Believed she could stir man's mind but not body

      b. Believed she had an odd way of looking at things

      c. Saw a wide smile take sting from rattlesnake mark over eye

IV. Described by people of the Bottom in 1939

  A. Said mark was Hannah's ashes

  B. Said mark had affected her from beginning

  C. Used Sula as scapegoat and blamed her for all woes

V. Described by Nel in year 1940 when Sula lay dying

  A. Saw a black rose once kissed by Jude

  B. Saw knife-thin arms and dark rose in bed

  C. Saw symbol of approaching death

VI. Described by Shadrack

  A. Recalled Sula's visit to his home

  B. Remembered she had a mark over her eye

  C. Knew she was a friend because had the mark of the "fish" he loved

  D. Recalled the belt and the tadpole-over-the-eye face

  E. Recalled seeing her on the table with the same little-girl face and the same tadpole over the eye

Topic #2

There are three main themes in traditional literature; these themes include the picaresque theme, in which the reader follows a character who travels or makes a journey; the reversal of fortune theme, in which the character has his or her situation in life changed; and the survival of the unfittest theme, in which a character who is not really equipped for survival is able to endure. How does the survival of the unfittest theme apply to the three characters appearing in the last chapter of *Sula?*

Outline

I. Thesis Statement: *The survival of the unfittest theme applies to* Sula *and the last two characters who appear in it. Shadrack is unfit psychologically yet he survives the cave-in and the ridicule of those in the Bottom. Nel is unfit emotionally because she defines herself through others yet she is able to outlive Sula.*

II. Applied to Shadrack

   A. Damaged on a battlefield in France

   1. Withstood the time in the hospital

   2. Withstood the time in jail and the sarcasm of the Bottom

   B. Had no visitors or friends except Sula

   C. Lost his fish—his recreation

   D. Used alcohol to extreme yet conquered the alcohol

   E. Led the people to the tunnel and yet did not die in the cave-in

III. Applied to Nel

   A. Defined herself through her husband, even though earlier said she was an individual, but evidence to contrary

   1. Said she never knew she had a neck until he commented on it

   2. Lonely when he left; later found lonely because of Sula

B. Allowed others to make her lonely

C. Defined herself through her children after husband left

D. Defined herself through circle after children left

Topic #3

Many conflicts are evident in *Sula*. Conflicts can be person against person, person against self, person against society, and person against nature. Which of these conflicts did Sula wrestle with in her life? Explain your answer. Be sure to include examples.

Outline

I.   Thesis Statement: *In Sula's life there exist all four types of conflict: person against person, person against self, person against society, and person against nature. These conflicts are evident as Sula moves from one stage to another in her life.*

Sula's Conflicts

II. Had person-against-person conflict

A. Wanted Nel to forgive her

B. Wanted Ajax to love her

C. Threatened by Eva who accused her of watching Hannah burn

III. Had person-against-self conflict

A. Cannot allow herself to settle into routine

B. Considers Hell to be sameness so tries to vary life

C. Never tells how Chicken Little dies

D. Like an artist with no art form

IV. Sula's person-against-society conflict

A. Was pariah of community

B. Encountered no rallying of community at sickness or death

C. Separated whites who bury and blacks who sing

       D.   Was object of rumors

       E.   Rejected because nonconformist

V.   Had person-against-nature conflict

       A.   Unable to fight death

       B.   Had to succumb to death

       C.   Found death did not hurt

Topic #4

Compare and/or contrast the concept of love for the following characters in *Sula*: Ajax and Sula, Eva, Jude, Nel, Helene Wright.

Outline

I.   Thesis Statement: *Love means different things to different characters in* Sula. *To Sula, love of Ajax means possession. Ajax refuses to be possessed. His only love is his mother and airplanes. To Eva, love is responsibility. To Jude, love is comfort for him. Nel takes her identity from the love of her husband and her children. To Helene Wright, the love of her daughter for a man means a wedding and the culmination of all that she was, thought, or did in the world; she drew her identity from that event.*

II.   Love to Sula

       A.   Act of love different from love itself

       B.   Possessiveness toward Ajax

III. Love to Ajax

       A.   Refusal to be possessed

       B.   Objects of love

           1.   Mother

           2.   Airplanes

IV. Love to Eva

       A.   Responsibility

       B.   Sacrifice of own safety to save Hannah

       C.   Exchange of leg to pay for needs of family

V. Love to Nel

    A. Loneliness after Jude's departure

    B. Identity of self derived from others

VI. Love to Helene Wright

    A. Object of daughter Nel

    B. Wedding of Nel the culmination of Helene's life

        1. All she had been

        2. All she had thought

        3. All she had done

Topic #5

Characters may be dynamic or static. A dynamic character changes, but a static character remains the same. Consider the characters of Helene and Nel. Which is static, and which is dynamic? Explain your answer.

Outline

I. Thesis Statement: *Helene is a static character and Nel is a dynamic one. Helene was a mother and guide to Nel; her entire life was committed to her daughter. When her daughter married, this was the culmination of Helene's life. She does not change. Nel, on the other hand, goes through several changes. She recognizes when she goes to New Orleans that she is an individual, but she forgets it along the way. She defines herself through others until the last chapter.*

II. Exhibits traits of a static character (Helene)

    A. Marries at the insistence of aunt

    B. Has daughter after nine years

    C. Culminates life at marriage of daughter

    D. Is concerned with appearances

    E. Shows no evidence of change

III. Exhibits traits of a dynamic character (Nel)

  A. Recognizes self as individual when goes to New Orleans as a child

  B. Defines self through husband

    1. Gives him comfort

    2. Does not realize had a neck until Jude comments

    3. Was not aware of self until affirmed by Jude

  C. Defines self through love of children when Jude leaves

  D. Becomes angry with Sula because Jude left

  E. Tries to define self through circle she joins

  F. Changes and forgives Sula in end

  G. Realizes she has always missed Sula—not Jude

  H. Makes changes in life (hopefully) as a result

Additional Topics

I. At several points in the book the narrators and characters make a distinction between the words *saw* and *watched*.

  A. Consider the following scenarios:

    1. When the two 12-year-olds walk down the street

    2. When Chicken Little drowns

    3. When Hannah burns

  B. Is *saw* or *watched* the appropriate term?

  C. What is the difference between the two?

  D. In your opinion did the men and boys *watch* or *see* the women and girls as they walked down the street?

  E. Did Nel *watch* or *see* Chicken Little drown?

  F. Did Sula, in your opinion, *watch* or *see* Hannah burn?

II. Writers use many devices to reveal the main character to their readers. They may show the character in action, reveal the thoughts of the character, show what the character says to others, show what others say to the character, and show the character in various environments. Which of these devices does Morrison use to expose Shadrack to her readers? Explain your answer.

III. Morrison uses many people to tell her story. Do you think one objective narrator could have presented the story better than a variety of narrators? Explain your answer.

SECTION FIVE

Bibliography

Blackburn, Sara. "Review of *Sula.*" *New York Times.* December 20, 1972, p. 3.

Carmean, Karen. *Toni Morrison's World of Fiction.* Troy, New York: The Whitston Publishing Company, 1993.

Century, Douglas. *Toni Morrison: Author.* New York: Chelsea House Publishers, 1994.

Kramer, Barbara. *Toni Morrison: Nobel Prize-Winning Author.* Springfield, New Jersey: Enslow Publishers, 1996.

Lambert, Walter J. and Charles E. Lamb. *Reading Instruction in the Content Areas.* Chicago: Rand McNally Publishing Company, 1980.

Marvin, P. H. "Review of *Sula.*" *Library Journal.* August 1973, 98:2336.

Morrison, Toni. *Sula.* New York: Penguin Books, 1973.

Otten, Terry. *The Crime of Innocence in the Fiction of Toni Morrison.* Columbia, Missouri: The Curators of the University of Missouri, University of Missouri Press, 1989.

Prescott, P. S. "Review of *Sula.*" *Newsweek.* January 7, 1974, 83:63.

Samuels, Wilfred D. and Cleonora Hudson-Weems. *Toni Morrison.* Boston: Twayne Publishers, 1990.